A SIMPLE GUIDE TO SPOKEN SINHALESE

THROUGH ENGLISH (A Revised Version)

A SIMPLE GUIDE TO SPOKEN SINHALESE

THROUGH ENGLISH (A Revised Version)

ALOYSIUS ASEERVATHAM

2023

Gotham books

30 N Gould St.
Ste. 20820, Sheridan, WY 82801
https://gothambooksince.com/
Phone: 1 (307) 464-7800

Published by Gotham Books (August 9, 2023)

ISBN: 979-8-88775-473-4 (P)
ISBN: 979-8-88775-474-1 (E)

Because of the dynamic nature of the Internet, any web addresses or links contained in this book may have changed since publication and may no longer be valid.

The views expressed in this work are solely those of the author and do not necessarily reflect the views of the publisher, and the publisher hereby disclaims any responsibility for them.

TABLE OF CONTENTS

DEDICATION

This book is dedicated to my loving brother-in-law:
the late Professor Dr. Wilfred Ferdinand,
and his wife the late Stella Ferdinand;
of Negombo, Sri Lanka.

FOREWORD

I regret not learning Sinhalese when I was young. Unfortunately, during the early days of my life in Sri Lanka, I didn't have the opportunity to learn Sinhalese, one of the two languages of the country. When I left Sri Lanka to work overseas, the opportunity to learn Sinhalese was not available.

During my extensive travels in Europe and Africa, whenever I met a compatriot who was a Sinhalese I had to communicate in English. I felt sad that I was unable to speak to a compatriot on foreign soil in a language from our home. On the many occasions I visited Sri Lanka, I was able to get by with English or with the help of a friend or a relative speaking in Sinhalese for me.

Every time I visited Sri Lanka I felt like fish out of water, whenever people around me was chatting away in Sinhalese. It was this experience that prompted me to write this guide with the help of some Sinhalese speaking friends in Brisbane. The purpose is to help those like me to be able communicate in Sinhalese.

Using my inherent ability for writing books, I resolved to write a simple guide to Sinhalese for the benefit of all those interested in learning Sinhalese, especially the tourists to Sri Lanka. Although most people converse in English, it is still beneficial to have some knowledge of Sinhalese when in the company of a Sinhalese only speaking crowd!

The secret to successful learning of Sinhalese is the mastery of the 'essential' Sinhalese vocabulary. Once a basic knowledge is obtained by studying this book, the reader can confidently study more advanced books on this language.

Aloysius Aseervatham   *Brisbane, August 2023*

ACKNOWLEDGEMENTS

I am deeply indebted to Jayantha Wickrematunge, the former convenor of Sri Lankan Radio Group of 4EB, Brisbane for his encouragement and input to this project. Without his help readily given in compiling a number of lessons, despite his busy schedule, this project would not have taken off the ground.

I am indebted equally if not more, to Chryshantha Senanayake of Brisbane for his tireless effort in helping me with the compilation of many lessons and for his constructive input.

The manuscript of this revised version was tidied up by my Brisbane friend Mark Perera and my daughter-in-law, Shubu Aseervatham, to both I am so very grateful.

This guide to spoken Sinhalese would not be an effective tool without an audiobook version. The audiobook helps the learner to pronounce Sinhalese words properly. In this respect also, my sincere thanks goes to Mark who was ably assisted by his wife, Chandra.

Last but not least, I am very grateful to my granddaughter Zuleikha Aseervatham for formatting the book in the manner I wanted and getting it ready for print in the shortest possible time.

AA

INTRODUCTION

This Guide to Spoken Sinhalese is intended for those who don't have any knowledge of the language but would like to become acquainted with it.

Lessons 1 and 2 cover the essential Sinhalese vowels and consonants and their mastery will lead to learning and understanding the common Sinhalese words used in conversations.

Lessons 3 and 4 gives an insight into the nature of Sinhalese and Lesson 5 looks at some simple phrases that are frequently used.

Each of lessons 6 to 55 is structured in a way to help learn some cardinal words under a specific category. For example, the lesson on describing colours in Sinhalese is under "Common Colours".

Every time a word is learnt in a lesson, it is used in a sentence. Other new words get introduced into the sentence. For example, if 'Yellow' is a specific word, the sentence, 'It is a *beautiful* yellow *flower*' introduces two new words.

The learner is encouraged to note the new words and then test whether they know the exact meaning of those words by doing the simple exercise that follow. Failing to identify the meaning shouldn't cause any concern as the answers to exercises are given at the back of the book.

An audio is available to help with pronunciation. By studying each lesson in the book and listening to the audio material for that lesson, the learner will gain confidence in speaking the Sinhalese sentences contained in that lesson.

The audio can be accessed via the website: www.aseervathambooks.com

LESSON 1

Sinhalese Vowels

There are vowels in Sinhalese as in any other language. We shall look at the twelve vowels in Sinhalese. A vowel has both a short sound and a long sound. It is important to know the difference.

We focus on the spoken language. We shall learn the sounds of 12 Sinhalese vowels through English in this lesson.

In order to know the exact sound of each vowel, it is recommended that the reader recognises the Sinhalese script it refers to. It is time well spent learning to recognise the script and even to write it. It helps to pronounce the Sinhalese words properly. Learning to write, the artistic Sinhalese scripts, can be fun indeed!

The twelve pure vowels:

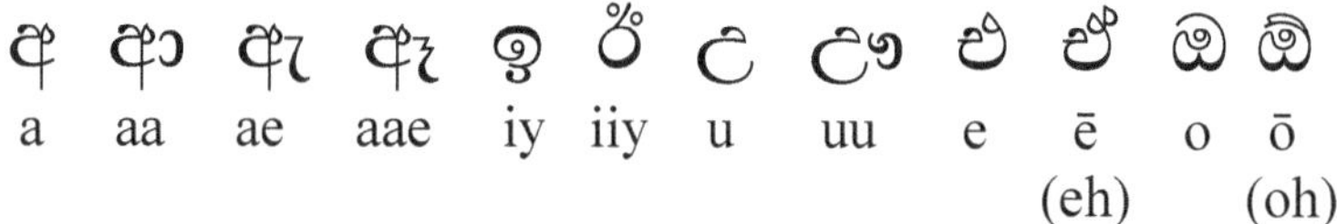

a	aa	ae	aae	iy	iiy	u	uu	e	ē	o	ō
									(eh)		(oh)

Note: The long sounds for එ and ඔ are denoted by 'eh' and 'oh' or ē and ō.

There are 58 letters in Sinhalese Language, but only 38 are used on a regular basis.

අ	a	(sound for 'a' is as for 'u' in c<u>u</u>p)
ආ	aa	(sound for 'aa' is as for 'a' in c<u>a</u>r)
ඇ	ae	(sound for 'ae' is as for 'a' in <u>a</u>pple)
ඈ	aae	(sound for 'aae' is as for 'a' in <u>A</u>nn)
ඉ	iy	(sound for 'iy' is as for 'i' in l<u>i</u>p
ඊ	iiy	(sound for 'iiy' is as for 'ee' in fr<u>ee</u>)
උ	u	(sound for 'u' is as for 'u' in pull)
ඌ	uu	(sound for 'uu' is as for 'oo' in pool)
එ	e	(sound for 'e' is as for 'e' in <u>e</u>gg)
ඒ	eh	(sound for 'eh' is as for 'a' in gr<u>a</u>ze)
ඔ	o	(sound for 'o' is as for 'o' in <u>o</u>nly)
ඕ	oh	(sound for 'oh' is as for 'o' in <u>o</u>ral)

EXERCISE 1:

1. Practice pronouncing the 12 vowels learned in this lesson.

2. Practice writing each Sinhalese Vowel five times.

3. Listen to the audio by visiting www.aseervathambooks.com

4. Practice writing the vowels to understand the differences between short sounding and long sounding vowels. Say them out loud as you write.

LESSON 2

Sinhalese Consonants

This lesson introduces the commonly used consonants in the Sinhalese language. In order to know the exact sound of each consonant, it is recommended that the reader recognises, as in the case of vowels, the Sinhalese character for each consonant. A mastery of the proper sounds will come with talking practice and listening to the audio.

ක්	+	අ	=	ක	ik + a	=	ka
ක්	+	ආ	=	කා	ik + aa	=	kaa
ක්	+	ඇ	=	කැ	ik + ae	=	kae
ක්	+	ඈ	=	කෑ	ik + aae	=	kaae
ක්	+	ඉ	=	කි	ik + iy	=	kiy
ක්	+	ඊ	=	කී	ik + iiy	=	kiiy
ක්	+	උ	=	කු	ik + u	=	ku
ක්	+	ඌ	=	කූ	ik + uu	=	kuu
ක්	+	එ	=	කෙ	ik + e	=	kay
ක්	+	ඒ	=	කේ	ik + eh	=	keh
ක්	+	ඔ	=	කො	ik + o	=	ko
ක්	+	ඕ	=	කෝ	ik + oh	=	koh

Pronunciation of a consonant changes when in combination with different vowels.

Commonly used Sinhala alphabets and their sounds

The table below gives the various commonly used Sinhala alphabets and an idea of the pronunciation of each alphabet.

Note: a long sound of an alphabet is denoted by a 'bar' above the alphabet, by writing the alphabet twice or by some other way! Observe and follow the method adopted in this book.

EXERCISE 2:

Practise writing and pronouncing each of the Sinhalese alphabets.

LESSON 3

Similar Sounding Alphabets

There are some similar sounding alphabets. Their wrong usage in a word would either make the word sound funny or give a totally different meaning.

Example 1:

The Sinhalese word for flower is mala මල and not malla මළ which means 'dead'.

The word for 'forehead' is na ll̲a la නළල with both 'll̲a" and "la". If written නලළ, the word would make no sense!

Similarly,

භ (bha) and බ (ba)

Example 2:

The Sinhalese word for dog is

ba̲l-laa බල්ලා and not bha l-laa භල්ලා

The word 'half' is bha-gaya භාගය and not bagaya බගය

ස (sa) and ශ (sha)

Example 3:

The word salli (money) is spelt with ස (sa) and not with ශ (sha)

The word '**santhosha**' (සන්තෝෂ) is written with both 'sa' and 'sha'

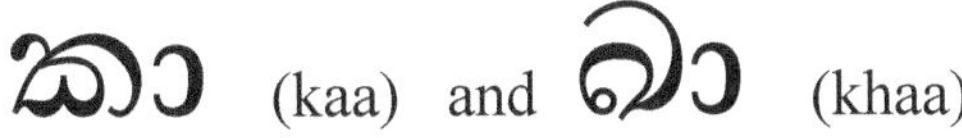

Example 4:

The word <u>Kaa</u>laya (Time) is written – කාලය

The name of a person, **Khaan** is written – බාන්

Example 5:

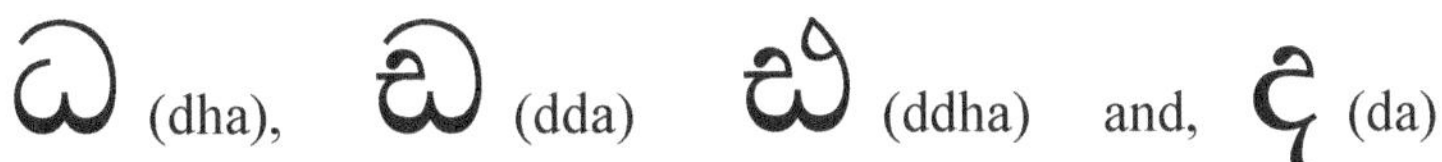

The word **Buddha** is written – බුද්ධ

The word **paaddam** (study) is written – පාඩම්

The word **muddhaya** (hard) is written – මුඩ්ය

The word **dannava** (know) is written – දන්නවා

EXERCISE 3:

1. Learn to recognise each Sinhalese alphabet encountered in this lesson from its pronunciation.

2. The Sinhalese words **mala** and **malla** mean 'flower' and 'dead' respectively. Write these Sinhalese words using Sinhalese script.

3. Differentiate each pair of letters below by pronouncing them properly:

    (a) ල ළ   (b) කා බා   (c) ධ ද
      (la) (lla)   (kaa) (khaa)   (dha) (da)

LESSON 4

Salient Aspects of Sinhalese

An English sentence does not get translated to Sinhalese, word to word in the same order. Some English words do not get translated but most English words have direct Sinhalese equivalents. The order of Sinhalese words may be changed in certain sentences.

How are you?	aayubovan, kohoma da?
What is your name?	Oyaagheh, nama mokkak da?
Where do you live now?	Daen oya inne kohe da?
How many children do you have?	Lamayi kee denek da?
This is a good book	Mekha hondha pothak
Do you want anything else, sir?	Mahaathmayaata vena mokkuth o'na da?
I must go now	Mama d'an yanna o'na

<h1 align="center">Plural words</h1>

A few letters get added to the singular word to give the plural word.

Singular		Plural	
bird	kuuruullaa	**birds**	kuuruulloh
cat	puusaa	**cats**	puusoh
dog	ballaa	**dogs**	balloh
elephant	aliyaa	**elephants**	ali
monkey	vanduuraa	**monkeys**	vanduuroh
snake	naya	**snakes**	nayi
flower	mala	**flowers**	mal
book	potha	**books**	poth

Wrong use of short and long vowel sounds change the meaning of a word.

Examples:

Dhaana	means	Alms giving
Dhana		Wealth
Kaalaya	means	Time
Kalaya		Pot
Maala	means	Necklaces
Mala		Flower

Wrong use of a double sound such as 'aa' or 'thth' changes the meaning of a word.

Examples:

Kola	–	Leaves
Kollaa	–	Boy
Atha	–	Hand
Aththa	–	Branch
Mala	–	Flower
Malla	–	Bag

Action words have specific endings. Some common endings are:

1. **karanava** – e.g., vaeda karanava (means working)

2. **venava** – e.g., vaadi venava (means sitting)

3. **gannava** – e.g., aha gannava (means listening)

4. **kiyanava** – e.g., sindu kiyanava (means singing)

5. **gahanava** – e.g., bera gahanava (means drumming)

Thiyenava and **innava** are two common endings that indicate presence, possession, or existence. Thiyenava refers to an object while innava refers to a person.

Examples:

I have a book.	Mata pothak thienava
My father is here.	Mageh thaaththa meththana innava

Present and Past Tenses

Observe the following carefully:

Present		Past	
Ask	ahanavaa	**Asked**	aehaevuvaa
Bathe	naanavaa	**Bathed**	naevaa
Bring	gehnavaa	**Brought**	genaavaa
Cry	anndanavaa	**Cried**	aenduvaa
Come	enava	**Came**	aavaa
Drink	bonavaa	**Drank**	bivvaa
Eat	kanava	**Ate**	kaevaa
Give	denavaa	**Gave**	dunnaa
Look	balanava	**Looked**	baeluvaa
Wait	innavaa	**Waited**	unnaa

Present, Past, and Future Tenses

Study the following examples carefully:

Present	**I speak**	mama kathaa karami
Past	**I spoke**	mama kathaa kalemi
Future	**I will speak**	mama katha karanneh

Present	**I love**	mama aadaraya karami
Past	**I loved**	mama aadaraya kalemi
Future	**I will love**	mama aadaraya karanneh

Present	**I ride**	mama padavami
Past	**I rode**	mama padevivemi
Future	**I will ride**	mama padavanneh

Query words

All query words end with "da"

Examples: mokkak da, o'na da, thiyenava da
thehruna da, nae'da?

Mixing English words in conversation

Modern spoken Sinhalese includes English words. It is sometimes convenient to use an English word instead of Sinhalese word when speaking.

Examples:

meh 'car' eka

ara 'market'

supermarket eka

airport eka

office eka

EXERCISE 4:

1. Familiarise yourself with all the new Sinhalese words encountered in this lesson.

2. Say the following in Sinhalese

    (i) bring   (ii) looked   (iii) wait
    (iv) speak   (v) love

3. Write each word above using Sinhalese scripts.

LESSON 5
Learning To Speak Sinhalese

In this lesson, we learn to say in Sinhalese some common everyday phrases using the English alphabet, moving from small sentences to lengthy ones. From the next lesson onwards, in each lesson we first learn the Sinhalese equivalents of a few English words under a specific category and then learn to say sentences in Sinhalese involving those words.

Simple common everyday phrases:

1. **I come**
   Mama enavaa

2. **You come**
   Oya enava

3. **Come this way**
   Mehe enna

4. **May I come in?**
   Mama athulata enna da?

5. **Have you eaten?**
   Oya kaeva da?

6. **Will you come?**
   Oya enava da?

7. **That bus is big**
   Ara 'bus' eka lokui

8. **My brother is coming tomorrow**
   Mag'e sahotharaya hettath enava

9. **I want to go now**
   Mama dan yanna o'na

10. **Give me something**
Mata mokak hari denna

11. **What else do you want?**
(oyaata) vena monavada o'ne?

12. **Why can't you come?**
oyaata enna bari ayi?

13. **We are planning to go next Sunday**
Api yanna hithan inne labana irida

14. **What different places will you visit?**
Oyaalak koyak kohetha balaanna yanne?

15. **He is coming at eight o'clock**
Eya enn'e attatta

16. **I will be going around seven o'clock in the morning**
Mama yanne udeh hathata vithara

17. **I get good income from that job**
maṭa eh rassaaven hoňda aadaayamak læbenavaa

18. **What other languages does that gentleman know beside Sinhalese?**
eh mahathayaa, sinhala ærenna mona bhaaṣaada danne vaa da?

19. **Do you have to go anywhere now?**
(oyaata) da'n kohehvath yanda thiyenava da?

20. **Tomorrow I am going to Peradeniya or Kandy.**
Mama heta Pehraadana hari Nuwarata hari yanava

EXERCISE 5:

1. Write the three sentences below in Sinhalese, using English scripts.

    (i)   My school holidays end tomorrow.

    (ii) I wish good teachers would come to teach me in my new class.

    (iii) The new Sinhalese teacher should be a clever one.

2. Read each Sinhalese sentence three times, pronouncing the Sinhalese words properly.

31

LESSON 6

The First, Second and Third Persons (1)

I, Me, You, We, They, He, She

English word	Sinhalese word written using English script	Sinhalese word written using Sinhalese script
I / Me	mama / mata	මම / මට
You	oyaa / oba	ඔයා / ඔබ
We / Us	api / apa	අපි / අප
They	ovun	ඔවුන්
He / She	aeya / ohu	ඇය / ඔහු

Some action words

English word	Sinhalese pronunciation using English	Sinhalese writing
Playing	sellam karanavaa	සෙල්ලම් කරනවා
Studying	igena gannava	ඉගෙන ගන්නවා
Sleeping	nidaagannava	නිදාගන්නවා
Crying	aňdanavaa	අඬනවා
Laughing	hinaa venavaa	හිනා වෙනවා

EXERCISE 6:

Say aloud in Sinhalese each English sentence given below.

English sentence	Sinhalese equivalent using English scripts
I am playing.	mama sellam karanavaa
I played.	mama sellam karaa
He (she) is playing.	ohu / (eya) sellam karanavaa
He (she) played.	ohu / (eya) sellam karaa
You are playing.	oyaa sellam karanavaa
You played.	oyaa sellam karaa
We are playing.	api sellam karanavaa
We played.	api sellam karaa
They played.	ovun sellam karaa
I am studying.	mama paadam karanavaa
I studied.	mama paadam karaa
He (she) is studying.	ohu / (eya) paadam karaa
You are studying.	oyaa paadam karanavaa
You studied.	oyaa paadam karaa
We are studying.	api paadam karanavaa
We studied.	api paadam karaa
They are studying.	ovun paadam karanavaa
They studied.	ovun paadam karaa
I am laughing.	mama hinaa wenevaa

I laughed.	mama hinaa wuna
He (she) laughed.	ohu / (eya) hinaa wuna
You laughed.	oyaa hinaa wuna
We laughed.	api hinaa wuna
They laughed.	ovun hinaa wuna

LESSON 7

The First, Second and Third Persons (2)

Mine, Your, Our, Us, Him, His, Her, Their, Them

English word	Sinhalese word written using English	Sinhalese word written using Sinhalese script
Mine	mag<u>e</u>	මගේ
Your	obage / oyaage	ඔබගේ
Our	apaghe	අපගේ
Us	apa / apita	අප
Him	ohuva / ohuta / ohuth	ඔහුව
His	ohuge	ඔහුගේ
Her	aeyge	ඇගේ
Their	ovunge	ඔවුන්ගේ
Them	ovunta	ඔවුන්ට

Say in Sinhalese, the English sentences given in the first column below:

English sentence	Sinhalese equivalent using English scripts
That book is mine	ara potha mageh

I studied with him	mama ohuth ekka iganagaththa
I am his friend	mama ohugeh yahaluwek
'Jayantha' is her brother	'jayantha' aeyageh sahodharaya
It is your duty	eka oyaaghe raajakaariyak
It is their home	eka ovunghe gedara
He brought it for us	ohu eka apita genavaa
I will go with them	mama ovun samaga yannam

EXERCISE 7:

1. What are the Sinhalese words for the following?

    (i) book   (v) home

    (ii) friend   (vi) brought

    (iii) brother   (vii) will-go

    (iv) duty

2. Read aloud the Sinhalese equivalent of each English sentence in the Table above.

LESSON 8

Query Words (1)

Who, When, Where, What, How, How many? How much?

English word	Sinhalese word written using English	Sinhalese word written using Sinhalese script
Who?	kavu da?	කවු ද ?
When?	kavadaa da?	කවදා ද ?
Where?	kohe da?	කොහෙ ද ?
What?	kumak da / mokak da / monawaa da	කුමක් ද ?
How?	keseh da / kohoma da	කෙසේ ද ?
How many?	kopamaṇa pramāṇayak da? / (kee denek da? / keeyak da?)	කොපමණ ප්‍රමාණයක් ද ?
How much?	kopamaṇa da? / kee ya da?	කොපමණ ද ? / කීය ද ?

Say in Sinhalese the English sentences given in the first column below.

English sentence	Sinhalese equivalent using English script
Who is he?	ohu kavu da? (eya kavu da)
Who is your father?	obeh thaaththa kavu da?
Who did you meet?	oba hamuvune kavu da?
Who do you want to meet?	obatta kavu da hamuwenna o'ne?

When did that happen?	e'ka kavadaa da une ?
When is he coming?	ohu enneh kavadaa da?
When are you coming?	oyaa kavadaa da enne ?
When are you going?	oba yanneh kavadaa da?
Where do you live?	oyaa koheda inne?
Where does he live?	ohu koheda inne ?
Where is the temple?	pansala koheda thienne?
What is your name?	oyaage nama mokak da?
What happened?	mokak da une?
What is your occupation?	oyaage rassaava mokak da?
What is the problem?	prasnaya mokak da?
What time is it now?	d'an welaawa keeya da?
How are you?	(oyaata) kohoma da?
How old are you?	oyaage wayasa keeya da?
How many children do you have?	oyata lamai kee dnek innava da?
How did this happen?	meka une kohoma da?
How many people are there?	(minissu) kee denek innava da?
How much is a kilo of rice?	haal kilo ekak keeya da?

EXERCISE 8:

1. What are the Sinhalese words for the following?

    (i) father   (ii) live   (iii) temple (iv) name
    (v) occupation (vi) problem (vii) time   (viii) children
    (ix) people

2. Read aloud the Sinhalese equivalent of each English
   sentence in the Table above.

LESSON 9

Query Words (2)

Is it not? Is it true? Is it a girl? Is it a boy? Do you understand?

English	Sinhalese equivalent written using English	Sinhalese equivalent written using Sinhalese script
Is it not?	nae da?	නේ ද
Is it true?	eya æththak da/ aeth tha da?	එය ඇත්තක්ද / ඇත්ත ද
Is it a girl?	eya gæhæṇhiyak da / kellek da?	එය ගැහැණියක්ද / කෙල්ලෙක් ද
Is it a boy?	pirimiyek da / kollek da	පිරිමියෙක් ද? / කොල්ලෙක් ද?
Do you understand?	thehrunaa da	තේරුනා ද?

Say in Sinhalese the English sentences given in the first column below:

English sentence	Sinhalese equivalent using English script
You are not telling the truth. **Is it not?**	oyaa kiyanne aeththa namei. nae da?
Malini had a baby. **Is it a girl?**	Malinita lamaek hambawuna. kellek da?

Mervyn is adopting a child.	Mervyn lamayekva hadhaganawa.
Is it a boy?	kollek da?
Go and have a look downstairs	pahala thattuuva geehilla balaanna
You have to continue to do all what I have told you.	mama kiyapu hæma dehma oyaa digaṭama karanna ohna.
Do you understand?	oyaaṭa thehreṇava da?

EXERCISE 9:

What are the Sinhalese words for the following?

    (i) truth   (ii) baby   (iii) adopt
    (iv) continue (v) told   (vi) understand

2.   Read aloud the Sinhalese equivalent of each English sentence in the Table above.

LESSON 10

Human Body Parts (1)

Head, Hair, Forehead, Eye, Ear, Nose

English word	Sinhalese word written using English	Sinhalese word written using Sinhalese script
Head	oluva	ඔලුව
Hair(s)	kes / hisakes	කෙස් / හිසකෙස්
Forehead	nalala	නළල
Eye(s)	aesa / ae s	ඇස / ඇස්
Ear(s)	<u>kana</u> / kan	කන / කන්
Nose	naasaya	නාසය

Say in Sinhalese the English sentences given in the first column below:

English sentence	Sinhalese Pronunciation using English script
He has shaved his head	eyaa konde (is) boogaalaa
I have to go for a haircut	mama konde kappa ganna yanna o'ne
She had 'pottu' on her forehead	eyaageh nalale thilakayak thibuna
Her eyes are very beautiful	eyaageh aes godak lassanayi

41

How is your ear problem now?	oyaageh kanne amaaruwa kohomada?
He has a big nose	eyaata loku nahayak thiyenava

EXERCISE 10:

1. What are the Sinhalese words for the following?

   (i) shave   (ii) haircut   (iii) beautiful
   (iv) problem   (v) big

2. Read aloud the Sinhalese equivalent of each English sentence in the Table above.

LESSON 11

Human Body Parts (2)

Mouth, Tooth, Tongue, Chin, Cheek, Neck

English word	Sinhalese word written using English script	Sinhalese word written using Sinhalese script
Mouth	mukhaya	මුඛය
Tooth (Teeth)	datha (da th)	දත (දත්)
Tongue	diva	දිව
Chin	ni ka ta	නිකට
Cheek(s)	kammoola (kammool)	කම්මුල (කම්මුල්)
Neck	bel la	බෙල්ල

Say in Sinhalese the English sentences given in the first column below:

English sentence	Sinhalese equivalent using English script
The child has something in the mouth.	lamayageh katte mokakhari thiyenava
She brushes her teeth daily.	eyaa dinapatha dath madhinawa
Show your tongue.	[oyaageh] di va pennanna
You have something on your chin.	[oyaageh] ni ka te monawahari thiyenava

You have a birthmark on your cheek.	oyaageh kambooleh upan lapayak thiyenava
She has a long neck	eyaata diga bellak thiyenava

EXERCISE 11

1. What are the Sinhalese words for the following?

    (i) child   (ii) something   (iii) brush
    (iv) birthmark   (v) long

2. Read aloud the Sinhalese equivalent of each English sentence in the Table above.

LESSON 12

Human Body Parts (3)

Nail, Thigh, Leg, Foot, Toe, Finger, Thumb

English word	Sinhalese word written using English script	Sinhalese word written using Sinhalese script.
Nail (s)	niya poththu	නියපොතු
Thigh(s)	kala vaa	කලවා
Leg(s)	ka k kula (ka k kul)	කකුල (කකුල්)
Foot(feet)	paada ya	පාදය
Toe(s)	aengilla (pa aengili)	ඇඟිල්ල (පා ඇඟිලි)
Finger(s)	aengilla	ඇඟිල්ල
Thumb(s)	ma pataengilla	මාපටැඟිල්ල

Say in Sinhalese the English sentences given in the first column below:

English sentence	Sinhalese equivalent using English script
I am cutting my fingernails	mama mageh niyapoththa kapanawa
He has hurt his thigh bone	eyaageh kalava asthi thuwala-wela (ridenava)
She has long legs	eyaageh kakul dhigai

You have to take care of your feet	oyaageh kakul balaaganna o'ne
He had hit his toe against a stone	eyaageh pa aengilla galeh ridenava
His thumb is swollen	eyaageh mapataaengilla edimila-wela

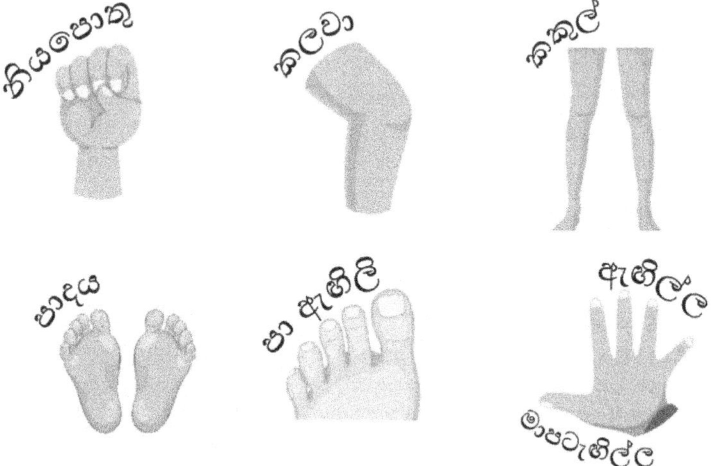

LESSON 13

Human Body Parts (4)

Chest, Breast, Armpit, Back, Bottom

English word	Sinhalese word written using English script	Sinhalese word written using Sinhalese script
Chest	papua	පපුව
Breast	tha-na-ya/ (piyayuru)	තනය (පියයුරු)
Armpit	kihilla	කිහිල්ල
Back	pita	පිට
Bottom	passa	පස්ස

Say in Sinhalese the English sentences given in the first column below:

English sentence	Sinhalese equivalent using English script
He has an infection of the chest	eyaata papuweh amaruwak thiyenava
She has breast cancer	eyaata thanayeh pilikawak thiyenava
He has a pain in his arm pit	eyaageh kihilla ridenava
He has a back problem	eyaata piteh amaaruwak thiyenava
His bottom is sore	eyaageh passa ridenava

EXERCISE 13

1. What are the Sinhalese words for the following?

    (i) infection (ii) pain (iii) sore (iv) cancer

2. Write each sentence in the table above in Sinhalese script

LESSON 14
Human Body Part (5)

Heart, Liver, Kidney, Stomach, Lung, Womb

English word	Sinhalese word written using English script	Sinhalese word written using Sinhalese script.
Heart	hada vatha	හදවත
Liver	ak maava	අක්මාව
Kidney	vaku gaduva	වකු ගඩුව
Stomach	bada	බඩ
Lungs	penahaḷu	පෙනහළු
Womb	garbhashaya	ගර්භාශය

Say in Sinhalese the English sentences given in the first column below:

English sentence	Sinhalese equivalent using English script
He is a heart patient	eyaa hadawath rogiek
He has liver cancer	eyaata akmaveh pilikawak thiyenava
She had stone in the kidney	eyaageh vakku ga dduva gal thibuna
What is wrong with your stomach?	[oyaageh] badeh amaaruwa mokakda?
His lungs are weak	ohuge pena hella duruwalai
She had a womb operation	eyaageh garbhashayeh saethkamak kala

EXERCISE 14

1. What are the Sinhalese words for the following?

    (i) patient   (ii) stones   (iii) wrong
    (iv) weak   (v) operation

2. Write each sentence in the table above in Sinhalese script

3. Match a picture to a word.

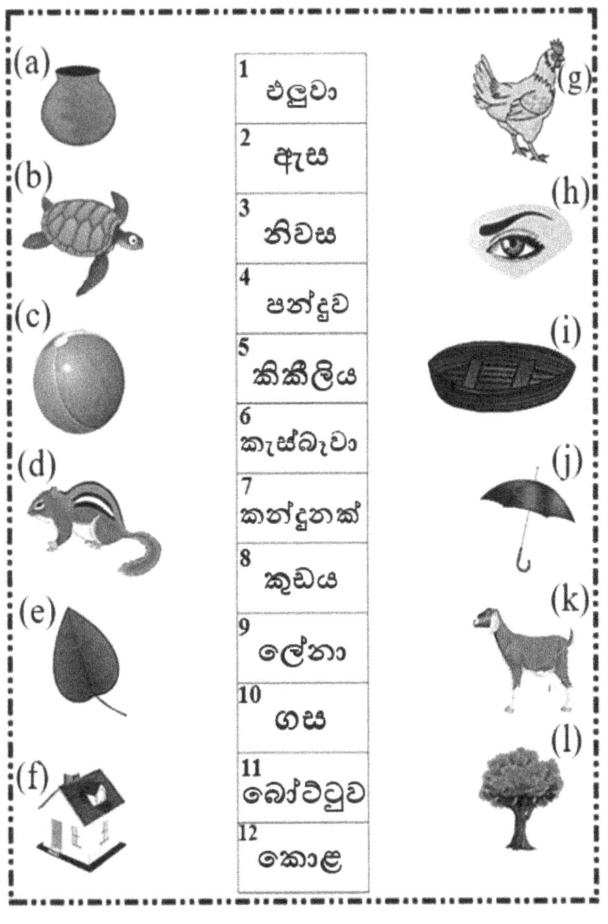

LESSON 15

Household Items

Chair, Table, Bed, Desk, Stool, Bookshelf, Door, Window

English word	Sinhalese word written using English script	Sinhalese word written using Sinhalese script
Chair	putuva	පුටුව
Table	mehsaya	මේසය
Bed	aenda	ඇඳ
Desk	liyana meshaya	ලියන මේසය
Stool	kudaa-bunkuwa	කුඩා බංකුව
Book shelf	thattuva / raakkaya	තට්ටුව / රාක්කය
Door	dora	දොර
Window	janeh laya	ජනේලය

Say in Sinhalese the English sentences given in the first column below:

English sentence	Sinhalese equivalent using English script
Sit on a chair	puṭuvaka vaaḍi venna
Keep it on the table	mehsaya uda thiyenna
This bed is uncomfortable to me	meh aeňda maṭa apahasui
Keep the two desks closer	liyana mehsa dheka ḷaňgin thiyenna

Bring that stool here	ara kuda bankuwa mehata gehenna
Keep it on the bottom-shelf	pahala thattuwe thiyenna
Close that door	ara dhora vahanna
Open the windows	janehl arinna

EXERCISE 15

1. What are the Sinhalese words for the following?

   (i) keep   (ii) uncomfortable   (iii) close   (iv) bring
   (v) bottom   (vi) closer   (vii) open

2. Write each sentence in the table above in Sinhalese script and read it aloud.

LESSON 16

Colours

White, Black, Blue, Green, Red, Yellow, Brown, Pink, Violet

English word	Sinhalese word written using English script	Sinhalese word written using Sinhalese script
White	sudu	සුදු
Black	kalu	කළු
Blue	nil	නිල්
Green	kola	කොළ
Red	rathu	රතු
Yellow	kaha	කහ
Brown	dumbhuru	දුඹුරු
Pink	rosa	රෝස
Violet	vayalat / dam	වයලට් / දම්

Say in Sinhalese the English sentences given in the first column below:

English sentence	Sinhalese equivalent using English script
I bought a white hat	mama sudu thoppiyak gaththa
Black colour is beautiful.	kalupaatta lassanayi
She wore a blue sari	eyaa nil paatata sariyak aenda

The garden was all green	waththa hondatama kola paattayi
He didn't stop the vehicle at the red light	eyaa rathu eliya pathu wunata vahanaya neweththuwe nae
It is a beautiful yellow flower	ehka lassana kaha malak
The brown (coloured) dog jumped over the fence	dumbhuru paatta balla vaetata uedin paenna
The pink dress suited her well	rosa paatta aedhuma eyaata hungak hondai
I like violet colour	mama dam paatata kemathiy

EXERCISE 16

1. What are the Sinhalese words for the following?

    (i) hat   (ii) bought   (iii) colour   (iv) garden
    (v) flower   (vi) dog   (vii) jumped   (viii) fence

2. Write each sentence in the table above in Sinhalese script and read it aloud.

LESSON 17

Greetings & Salutations

Good morning, Good night, How are you?, Thank you, Thank you very much, Happy Birthday, Happy Anniversary

English word	Sinhalese equivalent written using English script	Sinhalese equivalent written using Sinhalese script
Good morning	suba udhaesanak	සුභ උදෑසනක්
Good night	suba raadri yak	සුභ රාත්‍රියක්
How are you?	kohomada?	(ඔයාට) කොහොම ද
Thank you	isthu thiyi	ස්තූතියි
Thank you very much	bohoma isthu thiyi	බොහෝම ස්තූතියි
Happy Birthday	suba upan dinayak (vehvaa)	සුබ උපන් දිනයක් (වේවා)
Happy Anniversary	suba sangvathsarayak (vehvaa)	සුබ සංවත්සරයක් (වේවා)

Say in Sinhalese the English sentences given in the first column below:

English sentence	Sinhalese equivalent using English script
Good morning, Sir	suba udhae sanak mahaththmaya
Have a good night	suba raa thiriyak vehvaa

How are you, brother?	kohomada sahodaraya
I say thank you	mama isthuthi kiyanawa obata
I thank you very much for your hospitality	oyaageh sathkarayata mama bohoma isthuthi karanava obata
Wish you a happy birthday	oyaata suba upan dinayak pathanava
Wish you happy anniversary	oyaata suba sangvathsarayak pathanava
I wish you happy fiftieth wedding anniversary	oyaata suba panasweni vivaha sangvathsarayak vehvaa

EXERCISE 17

1. What are the Sinhalese words for the following?

    (i) sir   (ii) brother   (iii) hospitality
    (iv) wish   (v) wedding

2. Write each sentence in the table above in Sinhalese script and read it aloud.

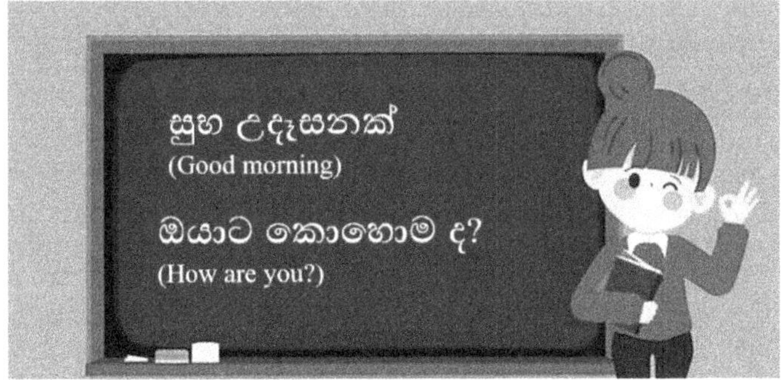

LESSON 18

Commands

Come, Go, Bring, Take, Walk, Run, Jump, Stop, Start

English word	Sinhalese word written using English script	Sinhalese word written using Sinhalese script
Come	enna	එන්න
Go	yanna	යන්න
Bring	genavaa	ගේනවා
Take	gannavaa	ගන්නවා
Walk	aevi dinna	ඇවිදින්න
Run	duvanavaa	දුවනවා
Jump	paninna	පනින්න
Stop	navath vanna	නවත්වන්න
Start	aarambha karanna	ආරම්භ කරන්න

Say in Sinhalese the English sentences given in the first column below:

English sentence	Sinhalese equivalent using English script
Please come soon	karunaakarala ikmanatta enna
You go home	oyaa gedara yanna
Take the short route	ketti paaren yanna
Walk fast	ikmanata avidinna
I am going to run	mama duvana yanawa
Jump over the fence	vaetata udin paninna
Stop here	meththana navathinna
Start now	d'an pattanganna

1. What are the Sinhalese words for the following?

   (i) please   (ii) soon   (iii) home   (iv) short
   (v) route   (vi) fast   (vii) fence   (viii) now

2. Write each sentence in the table above in Sinhalese script and read it aloud.

3. Match a picture to a word.

(a)    (1) ගස

(b) 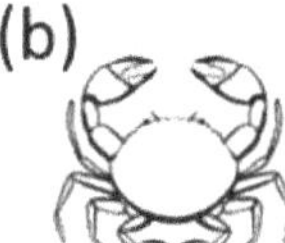   (2) කකුළුවා

(c)    (3) පන්දුව

(d) 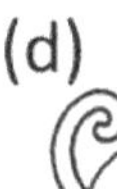   (4) මාළු

(e) 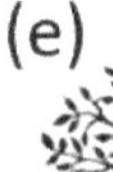   (5) වඳුරා

LESSON 19

Directions

Straight, Right side, Left side, Up, Down, North, South, East, West

English word	Sinhalese word written using English script	Sinhalese word written using Sinhalese script
Straight	kelinma	කෙලින්ම
Right side	dakuna pætta	දකුණු පැත්ත
Left side	vam pætta	වම පැත්ත
Up	dakvaa / uda	දක්වා
Down	pahaḷa / yatta	පහළ
North	uthuru	උතුරු
South	dakunu	දකුණු
East	naegenahira	නැගෙනහිර
West	batahira	බටහිර

Say in Sinhalese the English sentences given in the first column below:

English sentence	Sinhalese equivalent using English script
Go straight	kelin yanna
Turn right	dakunata harenna
Turn left	vamata harenna

Go up	udatta yanna
Go down	pahalata yanna
We live in the South side	api padinchi wela inneh dakuna paththeh
Jaffna is in the North of Sri Lanka	yapanaya thienneh siri lankawe uthureh
Sun rises in the East	hiru naginneh naegenahirin
Sun sets in the West	hiru basinneh batahiren

EXERCISE 19

1. What are the Sinhalese words for the following?

   (i) go   (ii) turn   (iii) live   (iv) side
   (v) sun   (vi) rises   (vii) sets

2. Write each sentence in the table above in Sinhalese
   script and read it aloud.

LESSON 20

Relatives (1)

Father, Mother, Son, Daughter, Older sister, Younger sister, Older brother, Younger brother.

English word	Sinhalese word written using English script	Sinhalese word written using Sinhalese script
Father	thaaththaa / piyaa	තාත්තා / පියා
Mother	ammaa / mava	අම්මා / මව
Son	puthaa	පුතා
Daughter	diyaṇhiya / duva	දියණිය / දුව
Older sister	akkaa	අක්කා
Younger sister	nangii	නංගී
Older brother	ayyaa	අය්යා
Younger brother	mallii	මල්ලී

Say in Sinhalese the English sentences given in the first column below:

English sentence	Sinhalese equivalent using English script
What is your father's occupation?	oyaageh thaa th thaageh rassaawa mokakda?

Where is your mother?	oyaage amma koheda inneh?
Is this your son?	meh oyaageh puthada?
How many daughters have you?	oyaata duvala keedenek innawada?
How old is your older sister?	oyaageh vaedimal akkaageh vayasa keeyada?
What is your younger sister doing?	oyaageh baala nangi monawada karanneh?
Is he your older brother?	eya oyaageh ayyaada?
How many younger brothers do you have?	oyaatta mallila kee denek innawada?

EXERCISE 20

1. What are the Sinhalese words for the following?

>   (i) occupation
>   (ii) how many
>   (iii) older
>   (iv) younger

2. Write each sentence in the table above in Sinhalese
   script and read it aloud.

LESSON 21

Relatives (2)

Uncle, Aunt, Sister-in-law, Brother-in-law, Grandfather, Grandmother

English word	Sinhalese word written using English script	Sinhalese word written using Sinhalese script
Uncle	maamaa	මාමා
Aunt	naendaa	නැන්දා
Sister-in-law	naaenaa	නෑනා
Brother-in-law	massinaa	මස්සිනා
Grand father	siyaa	සීයා
Grand mother	aachchi	ආච්චි

පවුලක්
(Family)

Say in Sinhalese the English sentences given in the first column below:

English sentence	Sinhalese equivalent using English script
Who is your uncle?	oyaageh maamaa kawuda?
Where does your aunt live?	oyaageh naen dah inneh koheda?
Where does your sister-in-law work?	oyaageh naae naa koheda vaedakaranneh?
Your brother-in-law seems to be a nice person	oyaageh mas sinna honda kenek vageh
Is your grandfather here?	oyaageh siyaa meththana innawada?
Does your grandmother live with you?	oyaageh aachchi oyath ekka jeevath wenawada?

EXERCISE 21

1. What are the Sinhalese words for the following?

   (i) work   (ii) here   (iii) nice   (iv) lived

2. Write each sentence in the table above in Sinhalese script and read it aloud.

LESSON 22

Relatives (3)

Husband, Wife, Family, Father-in-law, Mother-in-law, Granddaughter, Grand son

English word	Sinhalese word written using English script	Sinhalese word written using Sinhalese script
Husband	swaamipurushayaa	ස්වාමිපුරුෂයා
Wife	bhaaryaava / birinda	භාර්යාව / බිරිඳ
Family	pavulak	පවුලක්
Father-in-law	maamandhi	මාමන්ඩි
Mother-in-law	naendamma	නැන්දම්මා
Grand daughter	minhibiriya	මිණිබිරිය
Grand son	munhupuraa	මුණුපුරා

Say in Sinhalese the English sentences given in the first column below:

English sentence	Sinhalese Pronunciation using English script
Sunil is her husband.	Sunil, eyaageh swaamii purusshaya

Suraj came with his wife.	Suraj, eyaageh birindha ekka aaveh
They are a united family.	ovun ekamuthu pavulak
His father-in-law lives here.	ovungeh maamaandhi meheh jeevath venava
Her mother-in-law died last year.	eyaageh nandhamma giya avuruddheh maeruna.
Piyadasa has two beautiful granddaughters.	Piyadasata lassana mini biriyan dedenek innava
Ranjit loves his grandson a lot.	Ranjit eyaageh muunuu buraata godak aadarei

EXERCISE 22

1. What are the Sinhalese words for the following?

    (i) came   (ii) united

    (iii) died   (iv) beautiful

    (v) loves   (vi) lot

2. Write each sentence in the table above in Sinhalese script and read it aloud.

LESSON 23

At The Post Office

Post office, Letter, Parcel, Stamp, Envelope, Address

English word	Sinhalese word written using English script	Sinhalese word written using Sinhalese script
Post Office	thaepael kaaryaalaya	තැපැල් කාර්යාලය
Letter	liyuma / lipiya	ලියුම / ලිපිය
Parcel	parsalaya	පාර්සලය
Stamp	mudhdara	මුද්දර
Envelope	liyum kavaraya	ලියුම් කවරය
Address	lipinaya	ලිපිනය

Say in Sinhalese the English sentences given in the first column below:

English sentence	Sinhalese Pronunciation using English script
I am going to the post office	mama thaepael kanthoruwata yannava
I need to write another letter	mata thava liyumak liyanna o'neh
Please could you post this parcel?	karunaakkara, meh paarsalaya thaepal karanna
Please give me three Rs.50 stamps	karunaakkara, mata rupiyal panaheh mudhdara thunak denna
Please give me stamps for a registered letter.	karunaakkara, mata liyumak liyapaddinchi kirimatta mudhdara denna
I will write the postal address on the envelope	mama, lipinaya, liyuma kavarayeh liyannam

EXERCISE 23

1. What are the Sinhalese words for the following?

    (i) going   (ii) another   (iii) need
    (iv) give   (v) will-write

2. Write each sentence in the table above in Sinhalese script and read it aloud.

LESSON 24

Around The House/Hotel

Inside, Outside, Between, Beyond, Upstairs, Downstairs

English word	Sinhalese word written using English script	Sinhalese word written using Sinhalese script
Inside	aethul paeththa	ඇතුල් පැත්ත
Outside	pitta paeththa	පිට පැත්ත
Between	athara	අතර
Beyond	ehapaththe	එහාපැත්තෙ
Upstairs	udumahala / uda thattuuva	උඩුමහලේ / උඩ තට්ටුව
Downstairs	pahala thattuuva	පහළ තට්ටුව

Say in Sinhalese the English sentences given in the first column below:

English sentence	Sinhalese equivalent using English script
Go inside	aethulata yanna
Come outside	eliyata enna
You are caught in between	oya athara maedata ahuwelaa
It is beyond the gate	eka gehtuwen eha paththeh thiyenna
Go and have a look downstairs	pahala thattuuveh gihin balaanna
I am going upstairs	mama yanava uda thattuuvata
We have to go downstairs	apita pahala thattuuvata yanna o'na

EXERCISE 24

1. What are the Sinhalese words for the following?

    (i) caught   (ii) beyond
    (iii) look   (iv) going

2. Write each sentence in the table above in Sinhalese script and read it aloud.

LESSON 25

Counting (1)

One, Two, Three, Four, Five, Six, Seven, Eight, Nine, Ten

English word	Sinhalese word written using English script	Sinhalese word written using Sinhalese script
One	eka (ekkai)	එක (එක්කයි)
Two	deka (dekkai)	දෙක (දෙක්කයි)
Three	thuna (thunai)	තුන (තුණයි)
Four	hathara (hatharai)	හතර (හතරයි)
Five	paha (pahai)	පහ (පහයි)
Six	haya (hayai)	හය (හයයි)
Seven	hatha (haththai)	හත (හතයි)
Eight	ata (attai)	අට (අටයි)
Nine	navaya (navayai)	නවය (නවයයි)
Ten	dahaya (dahayai)	දහය (දහයයි)

Say in Sinhalese the English sentences given in the first column below:

English sentence	Sinhalese Pronunciation using English script
One country one nation	ekama rata ekama jaathiya

The two hearts are united	hadhawath deka ekamutuyi (hadawath deka ehkathu wuna)
A square has four corners	hathaves kotuwata mulu hatharak thiyenava
Five medals were won by Mohan	'Mohan' padhakkam pahak dinuva.
There are six sides for a die	daduketiyata paethi hayak thiyenava
Is Seven a lucky number?	hatha suba elakkamak da?
Eight churches are in this city	meh nagarayeh palli attak thiyenava
Nine planets affect the humans	grahalohka navayak minisunṭa balapaayi
Follow the ten commandments of God	deviyangeh dasa anapanath anugamanaya karanna

EXERCISE 25

1. What are the Sinhalese words for the following?

    (i) nation   (ii) heart   (iii) corner

    (iv) medal   (v) side   (vi) lucky-number

    (vii) church   (viii) planet   (ix) commandments

2. Write each sentence in the table above in Sinhalese
    script and read it aloud.

LESSON 26

Counting (2)

Eleven, Twelve, Thirteen, Fourteen, Fifteen, Sixteen, Seventeen, Eighteen, Nineteen, Twenty

English word	Sinhalese word written using English script	Sinhalese word written using Sinhalese script
Eleven	ekolahaa	එකොළහා
Twelve	dolahaa	දොළහා
Thirteen	dahathuna	දහතුන
Fourteen	daahathara	දහහතර
Fifteen	pahalova	පහළොව
Sixteen	daasaya	දහසය
Seventeen	daahatha	දාහත
Eighteen	dahaata	දහඅට
Nineteen	dahanavaya	දහනවය
Twenty	vissa	විස්ස

Say in Sinhalese the English sentences given in the first column below:

English sentence	Sinhalese Pronunciation using English script
Ten plus one is eleven	dahayata ekkak ekathu kalaama, ekholahai
Fifteen less five is ten	pahalawen pahak adu karama dhahayai
Twelve is less than fourteen	dolahaa, da-hatharata aduyi
Sixteen is greater than thirteen	da-saya, daha-thunata wada wediyi
Seventeen is an odd number	da-hatha, oththeh ilakkamak
Ten is an even number	dahaya, iratteh ilakkamak
Twelve items mean a dozen items	dusimak kiyanne do la hak

EXERCISE 26

1. What are the Sinhalese words for the following?

   (i) less   (ii) greater   (iii) odd   (iv) even   (v) dozen

2. Write each sentence in the table above in Sinhalese script and read it aloud.

LESSON 27

Counting (3)

Ten, Twenty, Thirty, Forty, Fifty, Sixty, Seventy, Eighty, Ninety, One hundred.

English word	Sinhalese word written using English script	Sinhalese word written using Sinhalese script
Ten	dahaya (dahayai)	දහය (දහයයි)
Twenty	vissa	විස්ස
Thirty	thiha	තිහ
Forty	hathaliha	හතලිහ
Fifty	panaha	පනහ
Sixty	haeta	හැට
Seventy	haeththaaeva	හැත්තෑව
Eighty	asuva	අසුව
Ninety	anuuva	අනූව
One hundred	siiya	සීය

Say in Sinhalese the English sentences given in the first column below:

English sentence	Sinhalese Pronunciation using English script
Ten and ten makes twenty	dahayai, dahayai ekatuwa vissai
Two times twenty is forty	vissa wedikarama utharaya hathalihayi
Eighty less thirty is fifty	asuwen thihak adu karama panahai
Five goes into hundred twenty times	siiyaa pahen beuwama vissayi
One hundred means a century	siiyak kiyanneh shathakayak
How much is thirty-six and forty-two?	thishayai saha hathalis dekai ekathukarama keeyada?
Not seven times seven but seven times seventy	hath warak hatha nemei, namuth hath warak haeththaaeva

EXERCISE 27

1. What are the Sinhalese words for the following?

       (i) makes   (ii) times   (iii) into

       (iv) means   (v) century   (vi) but

2. Write each sentence in the table above in Sinhalese script and read it aloud.

LESSON 28

Counting (4)

Learn to count from:

21 – 30; 31 – 40; 41 – 50; 51 – 60;
61 – 70; 71 – 80; 81 – 90; 91 – 100

The counting is similar to that from 11 – 20. Only the prefixes change as follows:

Twenty is **Vissa**

Numbers from 21 – 29, the prefix is "**visi**".

That is,
    visi-eka, visi-deka and so on.

Thirty is **Thiha**

Numbers from 31 – 39, the prefix is "**this**".

That is,
    this-eka, this-deka and so on.

Forty is **Hathaliha**

Numbers from 41 – 49, the prefix is "**hathalis**".

That is,
    hathalis-eka, hathalis-deka and so on.

Fifty is **Panaha**

Numbers from 51 – 59, the prefix is "**Panas**".

That is,
    panas-eka, panas-deka and so on.

Sixty is **Haeta**

Numbers from 61 – 69, the prefix is "**haeta**".

That is,
> **haeta-eka, haeta-deka** and so on.

Seventy is **Haeththaeva**

Numbers from 71 – 79, the prefix is "**haeththa**".

That is,
> **haeththa-eka, haeththa-deka** and so on.

Eighty is **Asuva**

Numbers from 81 – 89, the prefix is "**asu**".

That is,
> **asu-eka, asu-deka** and so on.

Ninety is **Anuva**

Numbers from 91 – 99, the prefix is "**anu**".

That is,
> **anu-eka , anu-deka** and so on.

One Hundred is **Eka Siiya**

EXERCISE 28

Practise counting from 1 to 100, ten times.

LESSON 29

Counting (5)

One hundred, Two hundred, Three hundred, Four hundred, Five hundred, Six hundred, Seven hundred, Eight hundred, Nine hundred, One thousand

English word	Sinhalese word written using English script	Sinhalese word written using Sinhalese script
One hundred	eka siiya	එක සීය
Two hundred	desiiya	දෙසීය
Three hundred	thunsiiya	තුන්සීය
Four hundred	haarasiiya	හාරසීය
Five hundred	pansiiya	පංසීය
Six hundred	hayasiiya	හයසීය
Seven hundred	hathsiiya	හත්සීය
Eight hundred	attasiiya	අත්තසීය
Nine hundred	navasiiya	නවසීය
One thousand	daahaa	දාහා

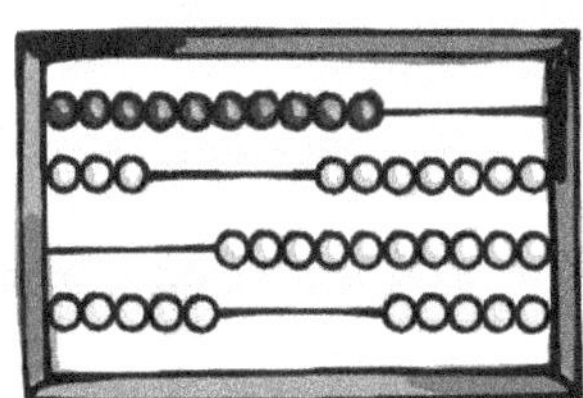

Say in Sinhalese the English sentences given in the first column below:

English sentence	Sinhalese Pronunciation using English script
One hundred and fifty percent	siiyata ekasiya panahaka prathishathayak
Two hundred and twenty runs	lakunu desiiya vissai
Two hundred years' old	awurudhu desiiak parana
Four hundred years ago	awurudu harasiyyakata kalin (issara)
There are six hundred students	lamayi hayasiyyak sitinava
Seven hundred entrance tickets were sold	praweesha pathra hathsiyyak vikunala
The collection came up to nearly one thousand dollars	ekathuwa 'dollars' dahakata kittui
We are talking in thousands	api kaththaa karanneh dahas gananin

---

EXERCISE 29

1. What are the Sinhalese words for the following?

   (i) percent   (ii) runs   (iii) old   (iv) ago
   (v) students   (vi) sold   (vii) collection   (viii) nearly
   (ix) talking

2. Write each sentence in the table above in Sinhalese script and read it aloud.

LESSON 30

Counting (6)

**Ten thousand, Twenty thousand, Thirty thousand,
Forty thousand, Fifty thousand, Sixty thousand,
Seventy thousand, Eighty thousand, Ninety thousand,
One hundred thousand.**

English word	Sinhalese word written using English script	Sinhalese word written using Sinhalese script
Ten thousand	dhasa dahasa	දස දහස
Twenty thousand	visi dahasa	විසි දහස
Thirty thousand	this dahasa	තිස් දහස
Forty thousand	hathalis dahasa	හතළිස් දහස
Fifty thousand	panas dahasa	පනස් දහස
Sixty thousand	haeta dahasa	හැට දහස
Seventy thousand	haeththae dahasa	හැත්තෑ දහස
Eighty thousand	asu dahasa	අසූ දහස
Ninety thousand	anu dahasa	අනූ දහස
One hundred thousand (one Lakh)	ek laksayak	එක් ලක්ෂයක්

Say in Sinhalese the English sentences given in the first column below:

English sentence	Sinhalese Pronunciation using English script
One hundred thousand is called a lakh	siiyehva dahak kiyanneh laksha ekai

Ten lakhs make a million	laksha dahayak 'million' ekai
A thousand million is called a billion	'million' dahayak kiyanne 'billion' ekai
A million million is a trillion	'million' 'million'ayak kiyanne 'trillion' ekai
There are more than 26 million people in Sri Lanka	sri lankaweh milliona visi hayakata wadaa senaga innava
Hundreds of thousand Sri Lankans have gone to live in other countries	lakshayakata wadaa lankaweh minissu pita rata padinchiyata gihin thiyenava
There are many millionaires in Sri Lanka	lankaweh dasa lakshapathio godak

EXERCISE 30

1. What are the Sinhalese words for the following?

> (i) many
>
> (ii) more
>
> (iii) migrated
>
> (iv) countries

2. Write six numbers (of your choice) between 500,000 and 600 000 and say them aloud in Sinhalese.

LESSON 31

Place Counting

First, Second, Third, Fourth, Fifth, Sixth, Seventh, Eighth, Ninth, Tenth etc.

English word	Sinhalese word written using English script	Sinhalese word written using Sinhalese script
First	pala-veni	පළවෙනි
Second	de-veni	දෙවෙනි
Third	thun-veni	තුන්වෙනි
Fourth	haththara-veni	හතරවෙනි
Fifth	pas-veni	පස්වෙනි
Sixth	haya-veni	හයවෙනි
Seventh	hath-veni	හත්වෙනි
Eighth	atta-veni	අටවෙනි
Ninth	nava-veni	නවවෙනි
Tenth	daha-veni	දහවෙනි

Say in Sinhalese the English sentences given in the first column below:

English sentence	Sinhalese equivalent using English script
Out of the five children first three are males.	lamayi pas denagen, pala-veni thundena pirimi - lamai

I am the fourth born in the family	mama pavule haththara-veniya
'Silva' was the fifth one to arrive	pasveniyata - aaveh 'Silva'
Third place receives bronze medal	thamba padakkama labune thun-veni thanata
'Sunil' came second in the race	diveemeh - tharagayen 'Sunil' deveniyata - aava
He came first in the class	ohu panthieh palaveniya
What is the seventh item in the agenda?	vaedasatahaneh – hathveniyata thiyenneh mokakdha?

EXERCISE 31

1. What are the Sinhalese words for the following?

    (i) children   (ii) born   (iii) family   (iv) arrive
    (v) receives   (vi) race   (vii) agenda

2. Write each sentence in the table above in Sinhalese script and read it aloud.

LESSON 32

Telling The Time

Nine, Nine fifteen, Nine thirty, Nine forty-five, One twenty, Twelve, Two twenty-five, Ten to six, Twenty past eight, Eleven fifty, Quarter to ten, Half past five.

English word	Sinhalese word written using English script	Sinhalese word written using Sinhalese script
Nine	namaya	නමය
Nine fifteen	namayayi kaalai / namayayi pahaḷova	නමයයි කාලයි / නමයයි පහළොව
Nine thirty	namayayi thiha / namayayi maarayi	නමයයි තිහ / නමයයි මාරයි
Nine forty-five	namaya hataḷis paha	නවය හතළිස් පහ
One twenty	eka vissai	එක විස්සයි
Twelve	doḷos / dolohaa	දොළොස් /දොළොහ
Two twenty-five	dekai visipahai	දෙකයි විසිපහ
Ten to six	hayata dahayai	හයට දහයි
Twenty past eight	atta pasuvi vissai (attai-vissai)	අට්ට පසුවි විස්සයි (ඇට්ටි-විස්සයි)
Eleven fifty	ekoḷahai panahai	එකොළහයි පණහයි
Quarter to ten	dahayata kaalai	දහයට කාලයි
Half past five	paha pasuvi thihai (paha maarayi)	පහ පසුවි තිහයි (පහ මාරයි)

Say in Sinhalese the English sentences given in the first column below:

English sentence	Sinhalese equivalent using English script
What is the time now?	d'an velaawa keeyada?
What time does the show start	keeyatada darshanaya patan ganneh?
What time is he coming?	ohu enneh keeyatada?
She always keeps to time	eyaa nithrama velawata vaeda karana kennek
The match will start at half past seven	kridawa patan gannawa haththa pasuvee vinaadi thihata.
It is better to go half an hour early	paya bhagayakata kalin yana - eka hondai
My watch is running fifteen minutes fast	mageh oralosuwa vinaadi pahalawak vadyi

EXERCISE 32

1. What are the Sinhalese words for the following?

    (i) now   (ii) show   (iii) start

    (iv) coming   (v) always   (vi) match

    (vii) better   (viii) early   (ix) watch

    (x) fast

2. Read aloud the following.

ලෝකයේ බොහෝ රටවල් ජනවාරි 1 වැනිදා අලුත් අවුරුද්ද සමරනවා. එහෙත් අලුත් අවුරුද්ද පිළිගැනීම සඳහා විවිධ දින සමරන ලොව පුරා දින දර්ශන කිහිපයක් තිබේ. ශ්‍රී ලංකාවේ අලුත් අවුරුදු සැමරුම අප්‍රේල් 13 වැනි දින ආරම්භ වී 14 වැනි දින එනම් සිංහල හා දෙමළ අලුත් අවුරුද්දෙන් අවසන් වේ. මීන රාශියේ සිට (මීන රාශියේ) සිට මේෂ රාශියට (මේෂ ලග්නය) හිරුගේ ගමන මත පදනම්ව ශ්‍රී ලාංකිකයන් අප්‍රේල් මාසයේ නව වසර පිළිගන්නේ රතිඤ්ඤා, ගිනිකෙළි සහ සාම්ප්‍රදායික රසකැවිලි රාශියක් සමඟිනි.

lohkayeh bohoh raṭaval janavaari 1 vænidaa aluth avurudda samaranavaa. ehet aluth avurudda piḷigænīma saňdahaa vividha dina samarana lova puraa dina darśana kihipayak tibeh. śrī laṁkaaveh aluth avurudu sæmarum aprehl 13 væni dina aarambha vī 14 væni dina enam siṁhala haa demaḷa aluth avurudden avasan veh. mīna raaśiyeh siṭa (mina raaśiyeh) siṭa mehṣa raaśiyaṭa (mehṣa lagnaya) hirugeh gamana mata padanamva śrī laaṁkikayan apehral maasayeh nava vasara piḷiganneh ratiññaa, ginikeḷi saha saampradaayika rasakævili raaśiyak samaṅgini.

English Translation:

Many countries in the world celebrate the new year on 1st of January. Yet there are several calendars around the world that celebrate different days to welcome New Year. In Sri Lanka, new year celebrations start on 13th of April and end on 14th of the month, the Sinhala and Tamil New Year. Based on the sun's movement from the Meena Rashiya (House of Pisces) to the Mesha Rashiya (House of Aries) Sri Lankan welcomes the new year in April with a lot of firecrackers, fireworks, and a gourmet of traditional sweets.

LESSON 33

Common Words

No, Yes, Certain, Correct, Nothing, Everything, Something.

English word	Sinhalese word written using English script	Sinhalese word written using Sinhalese script
No	næta /naae	නැත / නෑ
Yes	ov	ඔව්
Certain	samahara	සමහර
Correct	niværadi	නිවැරදි
Nothing	kisivak næta	කිසිවක් නැත
Everything	siyalla	සියල්ල
Something	yamak	යමක්

Say in Sinhalese the English sentences given in the first column below:

English sentence	Sinhalese equivalent using English script
No, I am not going today	naae, mama ada yanneh nei
Yes, I will be meeting him tomorrow	ov, mama heta eyaava hamba venawa
I am pretty certain about that	mata ehka hondhatama nivaeradhi
There is no correct answer for that	ekata hari uththarayak nei
I have nothing to hide	mata hanganna kisivak nei

| He gives careful thought to everything | eyaa hae ma de ya k ma hondata parissamen hithanawa |
| There is something wrong with him | eyaageh mokak hari wereddak thiyenava eyaata |

EXERCISE 33

1. What are the Sinhalese words for the following?

    (i) today   (ii) meeting   (iii) tomorrow
    (iv) answer   (v) hide   (vi) careful
    (vii) thought   (viii) wrong.

2. Read aloud the following Sinhalese passage:

ශ්‍රේෂ්ඨ පරාක්‍රමබාහු, ලංකාවේ සිංහල රජතුමා, දිවයින එකම පාලනයක් යටතේ එක්සේසත් කර, බෞද්ධ පිළිවෙත් ප්‍රතිසංස්කරණය කර, ඉන්දියාවට සහ බුරුමයට සාර්ථක ගවේෂණ කණ්ඩායම් යැවීය.

śrehṣdha paraakramabaahu, laṁkaaveh sinhala rajatuma, divayina ekama paalanayak yaṭateh eksehsat kara, bauddha piḷiveth pratisaṁskaraṇaya kara, indiyaavaṭa saha burumayaṭa saarthaka gavehṣaṇa kaṇḍaayam yaeviiya.

English Translation:

Paraakramabaahu The Great, Sinhalese king of Ceylon who united the island under one rule, reformed Buddhist practices, and sent successful expeditionary forces to India and Burma.

LESSON 34

Months Of the Year

January, February, March, April, May, June, July,

English word	Sinhalese word written using English script	Sinhalese word written using Sinhalese script
January	janavaari	ජනවාරි
February	pebaravaari	පෙබරවාරි
March	maarthu	මාර්තු
April	aprehl	අප්‍රේල්
May	maeyi	මැයි
June	juuni	ජූනි
July	juli	ජූලි
August	agohsthu	අගෝස්තු
September	sæptæmbar	සැප්තැම්බර්
October	oktohbar	ඔක්තෝබර්
November	novæmbar	නොවැම්බර්
December	desæmbar	දෙසැම්බර්

Say in Sinhalese the English sentences given in the first column below:

English sentence	Sinhalese Equivalent using English script
It rains here in January	janavaari maaseh, mehe wessa thiyanava
February and March are busy months for me	pebaravaari maarthu maassawala hondama vaeda thiyennava

I am going overseas in April	mama aprehl maaseh – rata yanava
My birthday falls in the month of May	mageh upandinaya maeyi maaseh
June is the end of financial year for us	apita juuni maaseh 'financial year' eka avasaan venawa
July, August, and September will be very cold here	juli, agohsthu ha saeptaembar maasa hondatama seeththalayi
Christmas seems to start in October	naththal okthohbar maaseh endanma pattan-ganava
My mother in law's death anniversary comes in November	mageh - nandammageh marana sangvathsaraya novaembar maaseh thiyenen
The school holidays start here around mid-December	meheh eskooleh nivaadu davas pattam ganneh desaembar meda tharameh

---

EXERCISE 34

1. Write the Sinhalese words for the following and read them aloud.

   (i) rains   (ii) busy   (iii) overseas   (iv) birthday   (v) cold

   (vi) anniversary   (vii) mid   (viii) holidays   (ix) around

2. Translate the following into Sinhalese:

   The Christmas holidays for schools start during the last week of November.

LESSON 35

Days Of the Week

Sunday, Monday, Tuesday, Wednesday, Thursday, Friday, Saturday

English word	Sinhalese word written using English script	Sinhalese word written using Sinhalese script
Sunday	iridaa	ඉරිදා
Monday	saňdhudaa	සඳුදා
Tuesday	aňgaharuvaadaa	අඟහරුවාදා
Wednesday	badaadaa	බදාදා
Thursday	brahaspatindaa	බ්‍රහස්පතින්දා
Friday	sikuraadaa	සිකුරාදා
Saturday	senasuraadaa	සෙනසුරාදා

Say in Sinhalese the English sentences given in the first column below:

English sentence	Sinhalese Equivalent using English script
Sunday is a holiday for most people	iridaa hungak minissunta nivadu davasak
I have to meet someone early on Monday morning	sandhudaa udetta mata kenekwa hamba venna thiyanava
I want to watch the cricket match on Tuesday	mata ohneh angaharuvada cricket tharangaya balaanna
My flight is on Wednesday night	mageh guwan gamana thienneh badaadu raeta
Shall we go to a restaurant for lunch on Thursday?	api brahaspathindaa dawal kemata 'restaurant' ekata yamudha?

We can have the party on next Friday night	api - iilanga sikuraadaa raeta 'party'a damu
I am getting some visitors on Saturday	mata senasuraadaata amuththu waagayak ennava

EXERCISE 35

1. Write the Sinhalese words for the following and read them aloud.

    (i) holiday   (ii) someone   (iii) night   (iv) flights
    (v) lunch   (vi) next   (vii) visitors

2. Read aloud the following Passage:

ශ්‍රී ලාංකේය සංස්කෘතිය ජාත්‍යන්තර වශයෙන් ක්‍රිකට්, සුවිශේෂී ආහාර පිසීමක්, දේශීය වෛද්‍ය ක්‍රමයක්, බෞද්ධ කොඩිය වැනි ආගමික ප්‍රතිමූර්තිය සහ තේ, කුරුඳු සහ මැණික් වැනි අපනයන මෙන්ම ශක්තිමත් සංචාරක කර්මාන්තයක් සමඟ සම්බන්ධ වී ඇත.

sri   laankehya   samskṛtiya   jaatyantara vaśayen krikaṭh, suviśehṣii aahaara pisiimak, dehśiiya vaidya kramayak, bauddha koḍiya væni aagamika pratimuurtiya saha teh, kuruṅdu saha   mæṇik   væni   apanayana   menma śaktimat samcaaraka karmaantayak samaṅga sambandha vii ætha.

English Translation:

Sri Lankan culture is internationally associated with cricket, a distinct cuisine, an indigenous holistic medicine practice, religious iconography such as the Buddhist flag, and exports such as tea, cinnamon, and gemstones, as well as a robust tourism industry.

LESSON 36

Workers

Teacher, Priest, Engineer, Doctor, Lawyer, Nurse, Clerk, Accountant, Policeman

English word	Sinhalese word written using English script	Sinhalese word written using Sinhalese script
Teacher	guru varayaa	ගුරු වරයා
Priest	pujaka varayaa	පූජක වරයා
Engineer	inginehru	ඉංජිනේරු
Doctor	dosthara / vaidyavarayaa	දොස්තර / වෛද්‍යවරයා
Lawyer	nithijnayaa	නීතිඥයා
Nurse	hediya	හෙදිය
Clerk	lipikaru	ලිපිකරු
Accountant	ganakaa di kaarii	ගණකාධිකාරී
Policeman	polisiya / poliskaarayaa	පොලිසිය / පොලිස්කාරයා

Say in Sinhalese the English sentences given in the first column below:

English sentence	Sinhalese Equivalent using English script
He is a good teacher	eyaa honda guruvarayek
I have to see a priest	mata puujakavarayek balaanna o'neh

Ramani works as an engineer	Ramani injinehruvidiyata vaeda karann / Ramani injinehruvariyak lesa sehvaya karayi
I have an appointment with the doctor	mata, dosthara hamuvenna velaavak thiyanawa
I will have to consult my lawyer	mata, mageh nithijna yaagen upades ganna o'neh
Malini is the head nurse at the hospital	ispirithaaleh pradhaana hehdhiya 'Malini'
Banda is just a clerk	'Banda' saamanya lipikaaruwek
Suraj is a brilliant accountant	'Suraj' athi-daksha ganakaadi varayek
Police arrested Sunil yesterday	iiyeh polisiya 'Sunil' wa atadanguvata gattehya

EXERCISE 36

1. Write the Sinhalese words for the following and read them aloud.

(i) works	(ii) appointment
(iii) consult	(iv) hospital
(v) brilliant	(vi) yesterday

2. Write each sentence in the table above in Sinhalese script and read it aloud.

LESSON 37

Evils

War, Fight, Enemy, Murder, Kill, Assassinate

English word	Sinhalese word written using English script	Sinhalese word written using Sinhalese script
War	yuddhaya	යුද්ධය
Fight / Fighting	kalahaya / saṭan karanavaa	කලහය / සටන් කරනවා
Enemy	sathuraa	සතුරා
Murder	minimaerumak / ghaatanaya	මිනිමෙරුමක් / සාතනය
Kill	maerenavaa / maranna	මැරෙනවා / මරන්න
Assassinate	ghaathanaya karanna	සාතනය කරන්න

Say in Sinhalese the English sentences given in the first column below:

English sentence	Sinhalese equivalent using English script
The war needs to stop	yuddhaya nævætviya yutuyi
We must fight for freedom	api nidahasa wenuwen satan kala yuthui
He is not my enemy	ohu mageh saththurak nemey
He was arrested for murder	minimaerumakata ohu athadanguwata gaththa
Kill that poisonous snake	oya visakuru nayawa maranna

There was a plan to assassinate the President	janadhipathi maranna kumantranayak thibuna (janaadhipativarayaa ghaatanaya kiriimeh sælasumak thibuṇa)

EXERCISE 37

1. Write the Sinhalese words for the following and read them aloud.

    (i) stop   (ii) freedom   (iii) poisonous
    (iv) snake   (v) plan   (vi) president

2. Search 'YouTube' and listen to the nursery rhyme:

මගෙ පොඩි තාරා පී පී ගෑවා..
හොට රතු පාටයි ඇඟ සුදු පාටයි..
අර අර පේනා සීතල වතුරේ..
අත් තටු සල සල පීන පීන නෑවා.

Mage podi thaaraa – Pii Pii gaewa
Hota rathu patai – anga sudu patai
Ara ara pehnaa – seethala vathureh
Ath thatu sala sala– peena peena naewa

My little duck shouted, "Pii Pii".
Its beak is red, and its body is white.
It was bathing in the pond there, with cool water
While flapping its wings and swimming.

98

LESSON 38

Creatures (1)

Dog, Cat, Crow, Hen, Cock, Fly, Mosquito, Grasshopper, Rat, Squirrel.

English word	Sinhalese word written using English script	Sinhalese word written using Sinhalese script
Dog	ballaa	බල්ලා
Cat	ballalaa / poosa	බළලා / පූසා
Crow	kaputaa	කපුටා
Hen	kikiḷiya	කපුටා
Cock	kukulaa	කුකුළා
Fly	maessa	මැස්සා
Mosquito	madhuruva	මදුරුවා
Grasshopper	palaagiravaa	පලාගිරවා
Rat	miiyaa	මීයා
Squirrel	lehnaa	ලේනා

Say in Sinhalese the English sentences given in the first column below:

English sentence	Sinhalese Equivalent using English script
I had a dog as a pet for a long time	goda kaalayak, surathal ballek hitiya mageh la-n-ga

My wife adores cats.	mageh bahryawa harima adarey puusanta
I don't see many crows these days	meh dhawaswala waediya kaputan penna naae
Our hens laid lot of eggs	appei kikiliya godak biiththara daanavaa
I heard the cock crow this morning	mata aehuna kukula ada ude handalenava
Could you please kill that fly?	karunaakarala oya maessa maranna pulawanda?
Don't forget to apply the mosquito cream	mathaka aethuwa madhuru aalepanaya ga-ganna
I haven't seen a grasshopper for a long time	mataka aethi kalekin mama palaagiravek dhaekeh naae
I was enjoying the cat torturing the rat	mama sathutu una puussa miyata wadadena haeti balalaa
My son's favourite pet in Sri Lanka was the squirrel	mageh putha Lankaaaawehdhi itama kaemathi satha lehnaa

1. Write the Sinhalese words for the following and read them aloud.

    (i) long time   (ii) adore   (iii) laid

    (iv) eggs   (v) lot   (vi) please

    (vii) apply   (viii) torturing   (ix) pet

    (x) favourite

2. Search 'YouTube' and listen to the nursery rhyme:

කිරි සුදු හාවා පැන පැන ආවා
එළවළු කොටුවේ දළු කොළ කෑවා
දැක මගෙ පඹයා බිය වී වෙව්ලා
වැටට උඩින් උෟ පැනලා දිව්වා

Kiri sudu haawaa – Pana pana aawaa
Elawalu kotuweh – dalu kola kaewaa
Deka mage pambayaa – biya wee wewlaa
Watata udin uoo – panalaa diwwaa.

English Translation:

White rabbit was hopping in the garden and
eating all the young leaves of the vegetable plants.
It was scared when it saw the scarecrow, and it began to shiver.
Then it jumped over the fence and ran away.

LESSON 39

Creatures (2)

Cow, Bull, Goat, Pig, Fox, Rabbit, Deer, Lion, Elephant, Tiger

English word	Sinhalese word written using English script	Sinhalese word written using Sinhalese script
Cow	ela dena	එළ දෙන
Bull	gonaa	ගොනා
Goat	elluvaa	එළුවා
Pig	uuraa	ඌරා
Fox	nariyaa	නරියා
Rabbit	haavaa	හාවා
Deer	muuvaa	මුවා
Lion	sinhaya	සිංහයා
Elephant	aethaa / aliyaa (Female) (Male)	ඇතා / අලියා
Tiger	kottiyaa	කොටියා

Say in Sinhalese the English sentences given in the first column below:

English sentence	Sinhalese Equivalent using English script
My mother used to milk the cow every morning	haema udayama, mageh ammah ella denagen kiri dewwa
I heard a cock crow	kukulek handalenava mata ahuna
Bulls pull carts	gonnu, karaththeh adinnava
Goat meat curry is quite tasty	ellu mas 'curry' hari honda rahai
Pig is a filthy animal	uursa, jaraa sathek
You can see foxes on this road	meh paareh, narriyo dakina puluwan
I have a rabbit in my house	mageh gedara haavek innava
You could find deer in this forest	meh kaleh muuvoh innava
Shall we go to see the elephants bathe?	aliyo naanava balaanna yamuda?
Tigers and lions can be seen in the Zoo	koti saha singhayo saththu waththedhi balaanna puluwan

1. Write the Sinhalese words for the following and read them aloud.

(i) mother   (ii) every   (iii) cart   (iv) pull   (v) tasty
(vi) filthy   (vii) road   (viii) house   (ix) forest   (x) bathe
(xi) zoo

2. Read aloud the following.

ගෞතම බුදුරජාණන් වහන්සේ බොහෝ "බුද්ධිමත් තැනැත්තා" ලෙස සැලකූ අතර, ඔහුගේ භාවනාව තුළින් සාමය සහ ජීවිතයේ දුෂ්කර ප්‍රශ්න බොහොමයකට පිළිතුරු සොයා ගත්හ.

gautama   budurajaaṇan   vahanseh   bohoh
"buddhimat   tænættaa"   lesa   sælakū   atara,
ohugeh   bhaavanaava   tuḷin   saamaya   saha
jīvitayeh   duṣkara   praśna   bohomayakaṭa
piḷituru soyaa gatha.

English Translation:

Gautama Buddha was considered by many "the enlightened one" who, through his meditation, found peace and answers to many of life's hardest questions.

LESSON 40

Creatures (3)

Tortoise, Turtle, Spider, Snail, Leach, Frog, Lizard, Centipede, Snake

English word	Sinhalese word written using English script	Sinhalese word written using Sinhalese script
Tortoise/Turtle	kæsbǣvaa	කැස්බෑවා
Spider	makuluvaa	මකුළුවා
Snail	gollubellaa	ගොළු බෙල්ලා
Leech	kuudaella	කූඩැල්ල
Frog	gemba	ගෙම්බා
Lizard	huuna	හූන
Centipede	paththaehyaa	පත්තේයා
Snake	nayaa	නයා

Say in Sinhalese the English sentences given in the first column below:

English sentence	Sinhalese Equivalent using English script
We have a tortoise in our garden	appeh waththe ibbek innawa
There are spider webs all over	haemathanama makula dal thiyanava
There is a snail on the wall	athana biththiye gollubellak innawa
There are leeches in the forest	kaelayeh kudello innawa
There are many frogs near that pond	ara pokuna langa hariyata maediyo innawa

Here lizards are found everywhere	mehe haemathanama huuno innawa
Centipedes can be seen in Sri Lanka	Sri lankaaweh paththaeyo balanna pluwan
This jungle is full of snakes	meh kaelayeh godak nayi innava

EXERCISE 40

1. Write the Sinhalese words for the following and read them aloud.

 (i) garden (ii) webs (iii) wall
 (iv) pond (v) everywhere (vi) jungle

2. Read aloud the following passage:

ගාල්ලට නුදුරු ගමක උපත ලද නවකතාකරුවෙක්, කෙටිකතාකරුවෙකු, කවියෙක්, සාහිත්‍ය විචාරකයෙක් සහ රචනාකරුවෙකු වූ ගුණදාස අමරසේකර නූතන සිංහල සාහිත්‍යයේ ආරම්භක පියෙකු ලෙස සැලකේ.

gaallaṭa nuduru gamaka upata lada navakataakaruvek, keṭikataakaruveku, kaviyek, saahitya vicaarakayek saha racanaakaruveku vuu guṇadaasa amarasehkara nuutana siṁhala saahityayeh aarambhaka piyeku lesa sælakeh.

English Translation:

Born in a village near Galle, the novelist, short story writer, poet, literary critic and essayist Gunadasa Amarasekara is considered one of the founding fathers of modern Sinhalese literature.

LESSON 41

Crockery

Cup, Glass, Tumbler, Bottle, Plate, Spoon, Knife, Fork

English word	Sinhalese word written using English script	Sinhalese word written using Sinhalese script
Cup	koppaya	කෝප්පය
Saucer	piirisiya	පිරිසිය
Bottle	bohththalaya	බෝත්තලය
Glass	viidhuru	වීදුරු
Tumbler	bona viidhuruva	බොන වීදුරු
Plate	pingaana	පින්ගාන
Knife	pihiya	පිහිය
Fork	gaaeraeppuwa	ගෑරුප්පුව
Spoon	haenda	හැන්ද

Say in Sinhalese the English sentences given in the first column below:

English sentence	Sinhalese Equivalent using English script
Please get me a cup of coffe	karunakara mata kohppi ekkak ge'enna
Keep the cup on the saucer	meh kohppaya piirisiya uda thianna
I need a bottle of water	mata waththuru bohththalyak ayashshai
Give me a glass of milk	mata kiri viidhiruwak denna
Don't you have a metal tumbler?	oyaa langa 'metal' bona viidhuruvak thiyenawada?

Bring the food in a plate	kaema piingaanatta gehenna
I will eat with a fork and a knife	mama haenden saha gaaeruppuven kannam
Please give me a spoon	mata karunaakarala haendak denna

EXERCISE 41

1. Write the Sinhalese words for the following and read them aloud.

   (i) get-me   (ii) keep   (iii) give-me
   (iv) food   (v) will-eat

2. Read aloud the following passage:

ශ්‍රී ලංකාව එහි ස්වභාවික භූ දර්ශනය, මිත්‍රශීලී මිනිසුන් සහ පොහොසත් බෞද්ධ සංස්කෘතිය සඳහා ප්‍රසිද්ධය. රටේ ආගමික හා ඓතිහාසික වැදගත්කමක් ඇති බොහෝ ස්ථාන ලොව පුරා සංචාරකයින් ආකර්ෂණය කරයි.

śrī lankaava ehi svabhaavika bhuu darśanaya, mitraśiilii minisun saha pohosat bauddha sanskṛithiya saṅdahaa prasiddhaya. raṭeh aagamika haa aithihaasika vædagatkamak æti bohoh sthaana lova puuraa saṃcaarakayin aakarṣaṇaya karayi.

English Translation:

Sri Lanka is well known for its natural landscape, friendly people and rich Buddhist culture. Many places with religious and historic significance in the country attract tourists from all over the world.

LESSON 42

Vegetables

Onion, Chilli, Tomato, Potato, Cabbage, Brinjal, Okra, Beans, Radish, Cucumber, Drumstick

English word	Sinhalese word written using English script	Sinhalese word written using Sinhalese script
Onion	luunu	ලූනු
Chilli	miris	මිරිස්
Tomato	thakkaali	තක්කාලි
Potato	ala	අල
Cabbage	gohvaa	ගෝවා
Eggplant	vambattu	වම්බටු
Okra	bandhakkaa	බණ්ඩක්කා
Bean	bohnci	බෝංචි
Radish	raabu	රාබු
Cucumber	pipinna	පිපිඤ්ඤා
Drumstick	murungaa	මුරුංගා

Say in Sinhalese the English sentences given in the first column below:

English sentence	Sinhalese Equivalent using English script
How much is a kilo of onions?	raththu luunnu kilo ekkak kiiyada?
Green chillies add taste to the cabbage curry	gohvaa 'curry' ekkatta ammu miris dammama rassa wadivenawa
Okra and drumstick are my favourite vegetables	bandakka saha murungaa mageh priyathama elavului
Tomatoes are good for the heart	thakkaali, hardaya vasthuvata hondai
Today mum is cooking bean curry	ada, amma bohnci 'curry' ekkak uyanawa
We need some cucumber for the salad	apita saladayata pipingna avashai
Radish is readily available here	raabuu mehe hingai

1. Write the Sinhalese words for the following and read them aloud.

        (i) taste   (ii) favourite

        (iii) vegetables   (iv) heart

        (v) cooking   (vi) need

        (vii) here   (viii) readily available

2. Search 'YouTube' and listen to the nursery rhyme:

අන්න අතන කූඹි රැලක්: අන්න අතන කූඹි රැලක් ගුලක් බඳිනවා. මෙන්න මෙතන ෙවෙයො රැලක් හුඹස්බඳිනවා පුංචි උනත් උන් හැම ෙලාකු වැඩක් කරනවා පුංචි අපිත් එකතු ෙවලා වැඩක් කරනවා.

anna atana kuuṁbi rælak; anna atana kuuṁbi rælak gulak baṅdinavaa. emanna ematha evveyo rælak huṁbasbaṅdinavaa puṁci unath un hæma eloku væḍak karanavaa puṁci apith ekatu evvalaa væḍak karanavaa.

English Translation:

There see a group of ants building an ant hole. Here see a group of termites building a hill. Even though they are so tiny they do a great work. Let us get together and work like them.

LESSON 43

Fruits

Orange, Grape, Apple, Banana, Mango, Coconut, Jack fruit

English word	Sinhalese word written using English script	Sinhalese word written using Sinhalese script
Orange	dhodham	දොඩම්
Grape	midi	මිදි
Apple	aepal	ඇපල්
Banana	kesel	කෙසෙල්
Mango	amba	අඹ
Coconut	pol	පොල්
Jack fruit	kos	කොස්

Say in Sinhalese the English sentences given in the first column below:

English sentence	Sinhalese Equivalent using English script
I must buy some oranges today	mama ada kohomahari dhodham tikak ganna o'ne
Grapes are very expensive	mi-di godak ganan
Apples are good for health	sharira savukyayata aepal hondai

Banana is my favourite fruit	mageh priyathama palathura kesel
This is not the mango season	meh amba wareh nowei
Coconut milk adds taste to any curry	onema 'curry' ekakata polkiri ekathu karaama, rasaya vaediyi wenawaa
Jack fruit is very tasty	kos itaarasavat

EXERCISE 43

1. Write the Sinhalese words for the following and read them aloud.

      (i) buy   (ii) expensive   (iii) health

      (iv) fruit   (v) season   (vi) milk

2. Write each sentence in the table above in Sinhalese script and read it aloud.

LESSON 44

Seafood

Fish, Dried fish, Prawn, Crab, Squid, Cuttlefish

English word	Sinhalese word written using English script	Sinhalese word written using Sinhalese script
Fish	maalu	මාළු
Dried fish	karavala	කරවල
Prawn	issan	ඉස්සන්
Crab	kakuluvaa	කකුළුවා
Squid	podi buvallaa	පොඩි බුවල්ලා
Cuttlefish	daellaa	දැල්ලා

Say in Sinhalese the English sentences given in the first column below:

English sentence	Sinhalese equivalent using English script
Fish is generally good for health	maalu saamaanayen sawukkayata hondai
I love prawn curry	mama isso 'curry' ekata hari kaemathiyi
Most people like both prawn and crab curries	godak minisun issan saha kakulu 'curry' walata kaemathiyi
Dried fish is exported by Sri Lanka	Sri Lankawen karawala apanayanaya karanava
Cuttlefish is much tastier than squid	podi buvallanta wada daellan godak rassayi

EXERCISE 44

1. What are the Sinhalese words for the following?

     (i) generally   (ii) most-people   (iii) both
     (iv) exports   (v) tastier

2. Read aloud the following passage.

බුද්ධාගම හඳුන්වාදීමේ සිටම කාව්‍යය ශ්‍රී ලාංකේය සාහිත්‍යයේ වැදගත් අංගයක් විය. ඇත්ත වශයෙන්ම එය බෞද්ධ කාව්‍ය ශාන‍රයේ ඉතා වැදගත් කොටසක් දරයි. ශ්‍රී ලාංකේය සාහිත්‍යයේ මෙන්ම ශ්‍රී ලාංකේය කාව්‍යයේ විශාලතම කොටස සිංහල භාෂාවෙන් ද ලියා ඇත. කෙසේ වෙතත්, එහි සැලකිය යුතු කොටසක් අනෙකුත් ප්‍රධාන භාෂා තුනෙන් සමන්විත වේ; පාලි, ඉංග්‍රීසි සහ දෙමළ.

buddhaagama haňdunvaadīmeh siṭama kaavyaya śrī laaṁkīya saahityayeh vædagat aṁgayaki viya. ætta vaśayenma eya bauddha kaavya śaanarayeh itaa vædagat koṭasak darayi. śrī laaṁkehya saahityayeh menma śrī laaṁkehya kaavyayeh viśaalatama koṭasa siṁhala bhaaṣaaven da liyaa æta. keseh vetat, ehi sælakiya yutu koṭasak anekut pradhaana bhaaṣaa tunen samanvita veh; paali, iṁgrīsi saha demaḷa.

English Translation:

Poetry has been an important part of Sri Lankan literature ever since the introduction of Buddhism. In fact it holds a very important part in the genre of Buddhist poetry. As in the Sri Lankan literature, the largest part of Sri Lankan poetry is also written in Sinhala language. However, a considerable part of it consists of the three other main languages; Pāli, English, and Tamil.

LESSON 45
Meats

Beef, Mutton, Lamb, Pork, Chicken,

English word	Sinhalese word written using English script	Sinhalese word written using Sinhalese script
Beef	harak-mas	හරක්-මස්
Mutton (Goat meat)	e_llu-mas	එළු-මස්
Lamb	bæṭaḷu-mas	බැටළු-මස්
Pork	uuru-mas	ඌරු-මස්
Chicken meat	Kukul-mas	කුකුල්-මස්

Say in Sinhalese the English sentences given in the first column below:

English sentence	Sinhalese Equivalent using English script
This beef preparation is delicious	meh harak mas hadhapu vidiya honda rassayi
I prefer goat curry to lamb	mama e_llu mas 'curry' ekata vadaa kaemathi battallu mas 'curry' ekata
My friend won't eat beef	mageh yahaluwa harak mas kanneh nei
Pork is not eaten by many people	hungak minissu uuru mas kanneh nei

| My mother cooks very tasty chicken curry | mageh amma hungak rassata kuku<u>ll</u>u mas uyanava |
| We shall buy some chicken nuggets today | api ada 'chicken nuggets' ganimu |

EXERCISE 45

1. Write the Sinhalese words for the following and read them aloud.

        (i) delicious   (ii) preparation

        (iii) prefer   (iv) friend

        (v) eat   (vi) cooks

2. Write in Sinhalese, a sentence involving each of the words above.

(You may use the appropriate sentence as seen in the table above).

LESSON 46

Stationery

Pen, Pencil, Eraser, Ruler, Sharpener, Clip, Stapler

English word	Sinhalese word written using English script	Sinhalese word written using Sinhalese script
Pen	paena	පෑන
Pencil	pænsala	පැන්සල
Eraser (Rubber)	makanya	මකනය
Ruler	'ruler'	රූලර්
Sharpener	'sharpener' eka	ශාර්පෙනර් එක
Clip	'clip' eka	ක්ලිප් එක
Stapler	'stapler' eka	ස්ටේප්ලර් එක

Say in Sinhalese the English sentences given in the first column below:

English sentence	Sinhalese Equivalent using English script
Can I borrow your pen for some time?	mata oyaageh paaena tika velawakata ganna puluwanda?
Have you got a pencil?	oyaata paensalak thiyenawada?
Give me an eraser	mata makana kaellak denna
You will need a ruler	oyaata 'ruler' o'na venawa

Can you sharpen that pencil	oyaata puluwanda meh paensala uulkarana?
You must get yourself a pencil sharpener.	oyaa paensala 'sharpener' ekak ganna o'na
We need a stapler or a paper clip.	apita'stapler' ekak hari kadadasi 'clip' ekak o'na

EXERCISE 46

1.   What are the Sinhalese words for the following?

    (i) borrow   (ii) give me   (iii) need
    (iv) paper   (v) get-yourself

2. Write in Sinhalese, a sentence involving each of the words above.

(You may use the appropriate sentence as seen in the table above).

LESSON 47

Money Dealings

Cheap, Dear, Discount, Commission, Brokerage, Donation

English	Sinhalese word written using English script	Sinhalese word written using Sinhalese script
Cheap	laabha(i)	ලාභ
Dear	ganan	ගනන්
Discount	adukiriima	අඩුකිරීම
Commission	komis mudala	කොමිස් මුදල
Brokerage	'broker' gaasthuwa	'broker' ගාස්තුව
Donation	dan denava	දැන් දෙනවා

Say in Sinhalese the English sentences given in the first column below:

English sentence	Sinhalese Equivalent using English script
I bought this very cheap	mama mehka hari laabeta miladi gaththaa
Motor cars are not very dear	'motor car' echchara ganan nei
I received a very good discount	mata honda mila adukirimak laebuna

I had to pay a commission for that transaction	Mama, meh huwamaruwata komis mudalak gewwa
The brokerage fee for this transaction is very high	meh huwamaruwata, 'broker' gaasthuva hungak vaediyi
I made a big donation for that charity	mama eh 'charity' ekata loku dan denava (dimak) kalaa

EXERCISE 47

1. What are the Sinhalese words for the following?

     (i) bought
     (ii) received
     (iii) transaction
     (iv) high
     (v) big

2. Write in Sinhalese, a sentence involving each of the words above.

(You may use an appropriate sentence as seen in the table above).

LESSON 48

Institutions

School, College, Hospital, Church, Temple, Police Station, University, Airport

English word	Sinhalese word written using English script	Sinhalese word written using Sinhalese script
School	paasaleh (iskola)	පාසලේ (ඉස්කෝල)
College	viiduhala	විදුහල
Hospital	ispirithaalaya / rohala	ඉස්පිරිතාලය / රෝහල
Church	palliya	පල්ලිය
Temple	pansala	පන්සල
Police Station	polis sthaanaya	පොලිස් ස්ථානය
University	vishva vidyaalaya	විශ්ව විද්‍යාලය
Airport	guvan thoṭupaḷa	ගුවන් තොටුපළ

Say in Sinhalese the English sentences given in the first column below:

English sentence	Sinhalese Equivalent using English script
Which school does your son go to?	oyaageh putha mona iskolayatada yanneh?
I studied in two colleges	mama viduhal deka kata giya

How far is the nearest hospital from your home?	oyaageh gedara eden langama ispirithaleta kopamana durak thiyenawada?
Is there a catholic church around here?	meh langa katholika palliyak thienewada?
I see many protestant churches here	mehe, reparamadu aagameh palli keepayak mata pehnawa
There is a Buddhist temple at the end of this road	meh, paara anthimatta bauddha pansalak thiyenava
The police station is quite far from here	polis isthaanayata meththana sita godak duurai
Kusuma is a lecturer at the Colombo University	Kusuma kolamba vishva vithyaalayeh kathachaarya wariyak
We have a very big airport.	apita godak loku guwan thotupalak thiyenava

---

EXERCISE 48

1. What are the Sinhalese words for the following?

   (i) studied   (ii) many   (iii) far
   (iv) churches   (v) lecturer   (vi) very big

2. Write in Sinhalese, a sentence involving each of the words above.

   (You may use an appropriate sentence as seen in the table above).

LESSON 49

Modes of Transport

Car, Train, Bus, Coach, Plane, Helicopter

English word	Sinhalese word written using English script	Sinhalese word written using Sinhalese script
Car	mohṭar ratha	මෝටර්රථ
Train	kohchchiya / dumriya	කෝච්චිය / දුම්රිය
Bus (Coach)	bas	බස්
Plane	guvanyaanaya	ගුවන් යානය
Helicopter	helicopter eka / helikopṭaraya	හෙලිකොප්ටර් එක / හෙලිකොප්ටරය

Say in Sinhalese the English sentences given in the first column below:

English sentence	Sinhalese Equivalent using English script
I bought a new car last week	giya sumanneh mama aluth car ekak gaththaa
I go by the 7.30 AM train to work	mama udeh hathahamaareh kohchiyen waedata yanava
Is there a bus to Colombo from here?	meththana indala bus ekak thiyenavada kolambata yanna?
My brother is arriving today by plane	mageh sahodharaya ada paminenawa guwanyanayen

124

| I enjoyed the helicopter ride yesterday | eeyeh mama 'helikopṭaraya ride' ekeng sathutu wuna |

EXERCISE 49

1. What are the Sinhalese words for the following?

>   (i) last week
>   (ii) from here
>   (iii) arriving
>   (iv) enjoyed

2. Write in Sinhalese, a sentence involving each of the words above.

    (You may use an appropriate sentence as seen in the table above).

LESSON 50

Locations

Town, Village, City, Country, Rural, Urban

English word	Sinhalese word written using English script	Sinhalese word written using Sinhalese script
Town	nagaraya	නගරය
Village	gama	ගම
City	maha nagaraya	මහ නගරය
Country	raṭa	රට
Rural	gambada	ගම්බද
Urban	naagarika / nagarbada	නාගරික / නගරබද

Say in Sinhalese the English sentences given in the first column below:

English sentence	Sinhalese Equivalent using English script
I grew up in a small town	mama hadhiwadune kudaa nagarayaka
Mark is from a small village near Kandy	'Mark' nuwarata kittu gamaka kenek
There is a lot of fun activity in the city at nights	raeta nagarayeh godak vinodha dewal siddhawenaya
Our country is quite peaceful	appeh rata godak saamakami

The people in the rural areas have a distinct culture	gambanda minissunta owunataaavenika sanskruthiyak thiyenava
Most people like to work in the urban areas.	godak minissu nagarabada vaeda karanna kaemathiyi

---

EXERCISE 50

1. What are the Sinhalese words for the following?

> (i) small
>
> (ii) activity
>
> (iii) peaceful
>
> (iv) culture
>
> (v) work

2. Write in Sinhalese, a sentence involving each of the words.

   (You may use an appropriate sentence as seen in the table above).

3. Read aloud the following:

ශ්‍රී ලාංකීය ඉතිහාසයට ආලෝකයක් දෙන මහා කාව්‍යයක් වන මහාවංශයේ සංයුතිය සාමාන්‍යයෙන් ආරෝපණය කර ඇත්තේ අනුරාධපුර මහාවිහාර විහාරස්ථානයේ බෞද්ධ භික්ෂුවක් වන මහානාම මහා තෙරුන් වහන්සේට ය. ඔහු ක්‍රිස්තු වර්ෂ 5 වැනි සියවසේ දෙවන භාගයේදී රජකම් කළ ශ්‍රී ලාංකික රජෙකු වූ ධාතුසේනගේ

මාමා කෙනෙක් ද විය. ක්‍රිස්තු වර්ෂ 4 වැනි සියවසේදී පමණ සම්පාදනය කරන ලද දීපවංශය ('දිවයිනේ වංශකතාව' යන්නෙහි තේරුම) මහාවංශය දැඩි ලෙස බලපෑවේය.

śrii laaṁkiiya itihaasayaṭa aalohkayak dena mahaa kaavyayak vana mahaavaṁśayeh saṁyutiya saamaanyayen aarohpaṇaya kara ætteh anuraadhapura mahaaavihaara vihaarasthaanayeh bauddha bhikṣuvak vana mahaanaama mahaa terun vahansehṭa ya. ohu kristu varṣa 5 væni siyavaseh devana bhaagayehdii rajakam kaḷa śrii laaṁkika rajeku vuh dhaatusehnageh maamaa kenek da viya. kristu varṣa 4 væni siyavasehdii pamaṇa sampaadanaya karana lada diipavaṁśaya ('divayineh vaṁśakataava' yannehi tehruma) mahaavaṁśaya dæḍi lesa balapǣvehya.

English Translation:

The composition of the Mahavamsa, an epic poem that sheds Light on Sri Lankan History is generally attributed to Mahanama Maha Thera, a Buddhist monk at the Mahavihara temple of Anuradhapura. He was also an uncle of Dhatusena, a Sri Lankan king who reigned during the second half of the 5 th century AD. The Mahavamsa was heavily influenced by the Dipavamsa (meaning 'Chronicle of the Island'), which was compiled around the 4th century AD.

LESSON 51

Gardens

Garden, Park, Grass, Plant, Weed, Flower

English word	Sinhalese word written using English script	Sinhalese word written using Sinhalese script
Garden	vaththa	වත්ත
Park	udyaanaya	උද්‍යානය
Grass	thanhakolla	තණකොළ
Plant	pælaya	පැලය
Weed	val pælaaeti	වල් පැලෑටි
Flower	mala	මල

Say in Sinhalese the English sentences given in the first column below:

English sentence	Sinhalese Pronunciation using English script
You have a beautiful front garden	oyaata lassana essaraha vaththak thiyenava
There is a public park near our house	apeh gedara langa, podhu udyanayak, thiyenava
That grass looks very nice	eh thannakolla godak lassanayi
There are many plants in your garden	oyaageh vaththeh paela godak thiyenava

I need to spray my plants with weed killer	Mata, paela walata val paelaaeti nashaka ihinna avashyai
I must buy some flowers for my wife	mama mageh bharayawata mal tikak mila dee gatha yuthumai

EXERCISE 51

1. What are the Sinhalese words for the following?

    (i) front   (ii) near   (iii) very nice
    (iv) garden   (v) weed killer (vi) wife

2. Write in Sinhalese, a sentence involving each of the words above.

    (You may use an appropriate sentence as seen in the table above).

3. Listen to the following **Baila song** Stanza "Kussi ammah Saaraa…." in the you-tube.

කුස්සි අම්මා සාරා, පෙරේරා
එක්කෙනෙක්ට ආදරය කළා
කුස්සියේ දොරෙන් ඔවුන් සිප ගන්නවා
මම දැක්කා
අනේ මගේ යාළුවා පෙරේරා, සාරාගේ
නහයට ගැහුවා
සාරා පෙරේරාට පයින් ගැසුවේ
දොරටය.

kussi ammaa saaraa, perehraa

ekkenekṭa aadaraya kaḷaa

kussiyeh dhoren ovun sipa gannavaa

mama dækkaa

aneh mageh yaaḷuvaa pereiraa, saaraageh

nahayaṭa gæhuvaa

saaraa pereiraaṭa payin gæsueh

doraṭaya.

English Translation:

Kussi Amma Sarah, was in love with one Pereira
I saw them kissing through the kitchen door
Oh, my friend Pereira, hit the nose of Saaraa
Saaraa kicked Pereira out the door.

(Baila is a form of music which originated centuries ago among the Portuguese Burghers in Sri Lanka. Baila songs are played during parties and weddings in Sri Lanka.)

LESSON 52

Spices

Mustard, Turmeric, Garlic, Ginger, Chilli powder, Curry Powder, Cinnamon

English word	Sinhalese word written using English script	Sinhalese word written using Sinhalese script
Mustard	aba	අබ
Turmeric	kaha	කහ
Garlic	sudu ḷunu	සුදුළුනු
Ginger	iṅguru	ඉඟුරු
Chilli powder	miris kuḍu	මිරිස් කුඩු
Curry powder	thuna paha	තුන පහ
Cinnamon	kuruṅdu	කුරුඳු

Say in Sinhalese the English sentences given in the first column below:

English sentence	Sinhalese Equivalent using English script
I use mustard for my curries	mama 'curry' walata aba paavichi karanava
Too much of turmeric is not good for health	godak kaha savukyata honda naehe
Garlic is available in the form of paste	sudu lunu thalapayak vidiyata ganna thienava

Ginger is an essential ingredient for Asian cooking	aasiyathikha kaema walata inguru aththyawashai
Chilli powder is used for most Indian curries	hungak indianu kaemawalata miris kudu yodanawa
Curry powder can be used with chilli powder	thuna paha, miriskudu samaga paavichikaranna puluwan
Cinnamon is used to give flavour to curries.	'curry' vasakaranna kurunda paavichikaranava

---

EXERCISE 52

1. What are the Sinhalese words for the following?

> (i) health
> (ii) essential
> (iii) most
> (iv) used
> (v) flavour

2. Write in Sinhalese, a sentence involving each of the words above.

   (You may use an appropriate sentence as seen in the table above).

ගම්මිරිස්   ලුණු

133

LESSON 53

Persons

People, Man, Woman, Children, Pupil, Student

English word	Sinhalese word written using English script	Sinhalese word written using Sinhalese script
People	mahajana	මහජන
Man	minihaa / mulikaya	මිනිහා / මූලිකයා
Woman	kaanthaavak / gaehaeniya	කාන්තාවක් / ගැහැනිය
Children	lamayi / dharuvan	ලමයි / දරුවන්
Pupil / Student	gohlaya / shiṣyayaa	ගෝලය / ශිෂ්යයා

Say in Sinhalese the English sentences given in the first column below:

English sentence	Sinhalese Pronunciation using English script
People are happy with the present government	meh aanduwata minissu kaemathyi
Man is the head of a family	primiya gruha mulikaya
Some women occupy very high positions in workplaces	samahara gehenu karyalawala ihala thanathuru wala sitanava
Children have too much freedom these days	dan kaaleh lamayinta uwamanawata wada nidahasa thiyenava

There are more than a thousand pupils in this school	meh iskoleh daahakata wada shishyo ennava
University students are under a lot of stress	vishva vidyala wala shishyan godak peedawen inneh

EXERCISE 53

1. What are the Sinhalese words for the following?

       (i) happy
      (ii) government
     (iii) family
     (iv) freedom
      (v) stress

2. Write in Sinhalese, a sentence involving each of the words above.

(You may use an appropriate sentence as seen in the table above).

3. Read aloud the following:

ක්‍රිස්තු පූර්ව 500 දී පමණ ඉන්දියාවෙන් ලංකාවට සංක්‍රමණය වූයේ සිංහලයන් නමින් හැඳින්වෙන ජනතාවකි. පුරාවෘත්තයට අනුව, පළමු පදිංචිකරුවන් විජය නම් මිනිසෙකු විසින් මෙහෙයවන ලදී.

ලංකාව මුලින්ම 1505 දී පෘතුගීසීන් විසින් යටත් විජිතයක් බවට පත් කරන ලදී, පසුව 1658 දී ලන්දේසීන් විසින්, පසුව 1796 දී බ්‍රිතාන්‍යයන් විසින් යටත් විජිතයක් බවට පත් කරන ලදී. අවසානයේ 1948 දී ලංකාව

kristu puurva 500 dhii pamaṇa indiyaaven
lamkaavaṭa samkramaṇaya vuhyeh simhalayan
namin hæňdinvena janataavaki.
puraavṛttayaṭa anuva, paḷamu padimcikaruvan
vijaya nam miniseku visin meheyavana ladhii.

lamkaava mulinma 1505 dhii pṛtugiisiin visin
yaṭat vijitayak bavaṭa pat karana ladii, pasuva
1658 dhii landehsiin visin, pasuva 1796 dhii
britaanyayan visin yaṭath vijithayak bavaṭa
path karana ladhii. avasaanayeh 1948 dii lamkaava
nidahasa labaa gaththehya. Ceylon yana nama
1972 dhii śrii lamkaava lesa venas viya.

English Translation:

About 500 BC, a people called the Sinhalese migrated to
Ceylon from India. According to legend, the first settlers
were led by a man named Vijaya.

Ceylon was first colonized by the Portuguese in 1505, then
by the Dutch in 1658, then by the British in 1796. Ceylon
finally gained independence in 1948. The name Ceylon was
changed to Sri Lanka in 1972.

LESSON 54

Office Accessories

Books, Basket, Tray, Bookshelf, Cabinet, Files, Folders

English word	Sinhalese word written using English script	Sinhalese word written using Sinhalese script
Book	potha	පොත
Basket	kuuḍaya	කූඩය
Tray	bandhesiya / thæṭi	බන්ඩෙසිය / තැටි
Bookshelf	poth raakkaya	පොත් රාක්කය
Cabinet	almaariya / maṇhḍala	අල්මාරිය / මණ්ඩල
Files / folders	gonu / fohlḍara (lipigonuwa)	ගොනු /ෆෝල්ඩර (ලිපිගොනුව)

Say in Sinhalese the English sentences given in the first column below:

English sentence	Sinhalese Equivalent using English script
I borrowed that book from the library	mama eh potha pusthakaalayan aragaththa
Put those documents in the basket	ara liyakiavili kuudaya athulata daanna
There are a lot of unattended letters in that tray	ara bandehsiyeh kiyawapu naethi liyum godak thiyenava

My bookshelf needs to be arranged properly	mageh poth raakaya piliwelakata us karanna o'na
We shall move the filing cabinet to the other corner.	api liyakivileh almaariya anith kohnata maarukaramu
Please open the relevant files	karunaakarala adala lipigonu viyurthu karanna
Keep all the new documents in this folder	okkoma aluth liyakivili meh lipigonuwata daanna

---

EXERCISE 54

1. What are the Sinhalese words for the following?

> (i) library
> (ii) documents
> (iii) unattended
> (iv) arrange
> (v) move
> (vi) files

2. Write in Sinhalese, a sentence involving each of the words.

    (You may use an appropriate sentence as seen in the table above).

3. Read aloud the following Passage:

දීපවලි (දීවාලි) යනු අයිපාසි / කාර්තිෙක මාසෙය් දින පහක් පුරා පවත්වන උත්සවයකි. ෙමම උත්සවය ඉන්දියාව, ශ්‍රී ලංකාව සහ සිංගප්පුරුව ඇතුළ ෙබාෙහෝ රටවල සමරනු ලැෙබ්. දීවාලි උත්සවය

සමරනු ලබන්නේ ජීවිතයේ අඳුර දුරු කර ආලෝකය ලබා දෙන උත්සවයක් වශයෙනි.

Deepavali (Diwali) yanu aipasi / kaartikai maasayeh dina pahak puraa pavatvana utsavayaki. mema utsavaya indiyaava, śrii lamkaava saha simgappuuruva ætuļu bohoh raṭavala samaranu læbeh. diwali utsavaya samaranu labanneh jiivitayeh aňdura duru kara aalohkaya labaa dena utsavayak vaśayeni.

English Translation:

Deepavali (Diwali) is a five-day festival in the month of October/November. This festival is celebrated in many countries including India, Sri Lanka and Singapore. Diwali is celebrated as a festival that dispels the darkness of life and brings light.

LESSON 55

Rates Of Motion

Slow, Fast, Slowly, Faster, Speed, Accelerate

English word	Sinhalese word written using English script	Sinhalese word written using Sinhalese script
Slow	semin / hemin mandhagaamii	සෙමින් / හෙමින් මන්දගාමී
Fast	ikmanin	ඉක්මනින්
Slowly	tikkak semin	ටිකක් සෙමින්
Faster	godak vehgayen	ගොඩක් වේගයෙන්
Speed	vehgaya	වේගය
Accelerate	vehgavath karanna (vehgaya vaedi karanava)	වේගවත් කරන්න (වේගය වැඩි කරනවා)

Say in Sinhalese the English sentences given in the first column below:

English sentence	Sinhalese Equivalent using English script
Please go slow	karunaakara hemin yanna
You speak so fast	oyaa kaththaa karanava hari ikmanata
They are slowly catching up with us	ovun harima hemin apita langa wenawa
Drive a little faster	tikkak vehgayen elawanna

Speed kills	vehgawathgamana maaraanthikai
There is no way we can accelerate on this road	meh paarehnam kohethma vehgaya vaedikaranna baae

---

EXERCISE 55

1. What are the Sinhalese words for the following?

> (i) speak
>
> (ii) drive
>
> (ii) catching
>
> (iii) little
>
> (iv) road

2. Write in Sinhalese, a sentence involving each of the words above.

(You may use an appropriate sentence as seen in the table above).

LESSON 56

Conversation (1) – Going Shopping

Friend:	Are you going shopping today? **oyaa ada kade yanawaada?**
Me:	yes. **ov.**
Friend:	What time are you planning to go? **mona welawatada oya yanna hitha gena inne?**
Me:	Say, around 10AM **ude dahayata vithara.**
Friend:	Would you be able to take me? **oyaata puluwanda mawath ekkagena yanne.**
Me:	Yes, sure. I will come at ten. **ov, puluwan. mama dahayata ennam.**
Friend:	That will be good. I will be ready at ten. See you later. **ehka hondayi. mama ude dahayata laesthi. velaa innam.**

LESSON 57

Conversation (2) – Getting a Taxi

Passenger: How much is the fare to go to the airport?
airport ekata kiiyak ganawada?

Driver: It is about Rs14,000/-
rupiyal daa hathara daahak vithara.

Passenger: How long would it take to get there?
kopamana velaawak gata wenwada ethanata yanna?

Driver: It would take approximately one hour and 45 minutes along Colombo Road.
kolamba paaren yanawanam aduma taramin peyay vinadi haththalis pahak vithara yanawa.

Passenger: Is there any faster route to get there?
ethanata yanna vena ikman paarak thiyenavada?

Driver: No, this is the quickest.
nehe, meka tamai ikman.

Passenger Okay, let's go
hondai. ehenam yamu.

Passenger:	Could you please turn to the right here and then to the left and stop at the entrance? **karunakarala, meththanin dakunata harawala ea – langata wamata harawala athulwana tenin nawatthanna?**
Driver:	Okay **hondai**
Passenger:	Thank you very much. **bohoma isthuthiyi.**
Driver:	Thank you and wish you a safe journey. **isthuthiyi. uba gamanak.**

LESSON 58

Conversation (3) – Checking in at the Airport

Airline staff:	Good morning, Can I have your ticket, please? **suba udesanak wehwa. karunakarala 'ticket' eka denna**
Passenger:	Please give a window seat. **karunakarala janellaya langa 'seat' ekak denna.**
Airline staff:	Possible. **puluwan.**
Airline staff:	Is there any baggage? **'baggage" thiyenavada?**
Passenger:	Yes, this suitcase and this carryon bag. **ov. meh 'suitcase' ekai, mei 'handbag' ekai.**
Airline staff:	Did you pack your bag yourself? **gaman malla asiruweh numbada?**
Passenger:	Yes. **ov.**

| *Airline staff:* | Is there any dangerous chemicals the bag?
**athuleh 'bag' eka   rasayana
drawya mokawat thieyanavada?** |

| *Passenger:* | No.
nehe. |

| *Airline staff:* | Here's your boarding pass, have a nice flight.
menna 'boarding pass' eka. Suba gamanak. |

| *Passenger:* | Thank you.
isthuthiyi. |

LESSON 59

Conversation (4) – Getting a Room in a Hotel

Hotel staff: Good evening, Can I help you?
Suba-sandewak. mata-oyaata udaw karanna puluwanda?

Guest: Yes please. I would like a room for the night.
ov. mata ada-raeyta kaamrayak avashai

Hotel staff: Would you like a single room, or a double room?
oyaa kamathi 'single room' ehakatada ehema nathinam 'double room' ehakatada?

Guest: A single room, please. How much is the room?
'single room'. Kaamarayakata - keeyadha?

Hotel staff: It's Rs. 14, 900 per night.
ekka raeyakata rupiyal daha- hathara-dahas namasiyyai -

Guest: Can I pay by credit card?
Mata 'credit card' ekken - gevanna puluwanda?

| *Hotel staff:* | Certainly. We take Visa, Master Card and American Express. Could you fill in this form, please**?** |
| | **ov. Api - baragannawa 'Visa', 'Master Card' saha 'American Express.'. Meh 'form' eka purawanna puluwanda?** |

| *Guest:* | Do you need my passport ? |
| | **oyaata, Mageh 'passport' eka avashada?** |

| *Hotel staff:* | No, just an address and your signature. |
| | **nehe, lipinaya saha oyaageh athsana - aeththi** |

| *Guest:* | *(fills out the form)* Here you are, the filled form. |
| | **menna, sampurnakarapu 'form' eka** |

| *Hotel staff:* | Here's the key for your room. Room number is 22 and it overlooks the beach |
| | **menna - kaamaraye yathuru. Kaamara ankaya visi deka kaamaraya muhuda paththatta muhunala thiennei.** |

| *Guest:* | Thank you very much. |
| | **bohoma – isthuthiyi.** |

| *Hotel staff:* | If you need anything, dial 0. |
| | **oyaata monovahari avashanam, anka binduwa amaththanna.** |

Guest:	*(calls room service)* I am calling from room 22. Could I please have a Black Label Whisky and a bottle of Port wine. **meh, kathakaranne kaamara anka visi dekken. Mata 'Black Label Whisky' ekak saha 'Port wine bottle' ekak ganna puluwanda?**
Hotel staff:	Yes Sir, order will be there in 10 minutes **ov Sir, vinaadi - dahayen 'order' eka evanna puluwan.**
Guest:	Thank you very much. **bohoma isthuthiyi**

LESSON 60

Conversation (5) – Having A Meal In A Restaurant

Waitress: Good afternoon, here is the menu for today, sir.
suba sandayawak, menna ada 'menu' eka mahaathmaya.

Customer: Thank you. What's today's special?
isthuthiyi, monawada ada vishehsha?

Waitress: Mutton Buriyani and vattalappam.
eealu-mas buriyani saha vattalappam.

Customer: That sounds good. I'll have that.
ehka hondayi, mama gunnam.

Waitress: Would you like something to drink?
oyaa kaemathida monowahari bonna?

Customer: Yes, I'd like a beer.
ov mama kaamathiyi 'beer' ekakata.

Waitress: (hands over the beer) Let me know when you are ready to have the meal.
mata kiyanna oyaa kaema kanna kaemathi welawata.

Customer: Thank you. Shall do.
isthuthiyi, mama kiyannam.

| *Waitress:* | Here is your meal sir. Enjoy. |
| | **menna mahaathmaya oyaageh kaema eka rasawindinna.** |

| *Customer:* | May I have the bill, please? |
| | **karunaakarala mata bila denna puluwanda?** |

| *Waitress:* | Here is the bill, sir. |
| | **menna bila, mahaathmaya.** |

| *Customer:* | Here is the money. Keep the change! |
| | **menna salli, maarusalli thiyaganna!** |

| *Waitress:* | Thank you. Have a good day! |
| | **isthuthiyi, aayubowan!** |

LESSON 61

Conversation (6) – Getting Traveller's Cheques

Forex Teller: Good Morning, how may I help you?
Suba udesanak, mata puluwanda oyaata udavu karanna?

Customer: I would like to cash some travellers' cheques.
mama kaemathi sancharaka chekpath keepayak salliwalata maaru karanna.

Forex Teller: In what currency have you got them? Can I have the cheques and your passport please?
mona rateh salli walinda thiyenneh? Karunaakarala mata chekpath tikayi 'passport' ekkyi denna.

Customer: Here you are, the travellers' cheques are in American dollars.
aa menna, sancharaka chekpath thiyenneh "american dollars" walin.

Forex Teller: How much are you cashing?
kochcharak salliwalata maarukaranna o'nada?

Customer: I would like to cash 300 American dollars
mama kamathi "American dollars" thun siyayak salliwalata maaru karala ganna.

| *Forex Teller:* | In what denominations would you like to have the cash?
koyi widihatada oyaata salli kola o'na caranna? |

| *Customer:* | Give me half in 5 thousand rupee notes, some thousand-rupee notes and the rest in 100's.
mata bhagayak Rupiyal pandahaseh nottu walin keepayak Rupiyal dahaseh nottu walin saha ethiri salli Rupiyal siiyeh nottu walin denna. |

| *Forex Teller:* | Could you please sign each cheque for me.
karunaakarala meh haema chekpathakma athsan karanna. |

| *Customer:* | O' kay.
hondai. |

| *Forex Teller:* | Here is the money. Have a nice day.
menna salli, suba dawasak. |

| *Customer:* | Thank you very much.
bohoma isthuthiyi. |

LESSON 62

Conversation (7) – Asking Directions To Super Market

Tourist:	Is there a supermarket around here? **meh langa'supermarket' ekak thiyenavada?**
Native:	Yes. There's one near here. **ov, meh langa ekak thiyenava.**
Tourist:	How do I get there? **mama kohomada ethanata yanneh?**
Native:	Proceed along this street. At the first traffic lights, take a left and go straight on. It's on the right. **meh paareh digatama yanna. palaveni 'traffic light' eken wamata hearila essaraata yanna eka dakunu paththeh thiyenava.**
Tourist:	Is it far? **hungak duurada?**
Native:	Not really. **echchara nehe**
Tourist:	Thank you. Much obliged. **oyaata bohoma isthuthiyi.**

LESSON 63

Conversation (8) – Shopping For A Shirt

Shopkeeper: Can I help you?
mata puluwanda oyaata udawwakkaranna?

Customer: Yes, I'm looking for a gent's cotton shirt.
ov, mama soyanawa pirimi kapu kamisayak.

Shopkeeper: What size are you?
mokakda oyaageh 'size' ekka?

Customer: I'm an extra-large.
mageh size eka 'extra large'.

Shopkeeper: How about this one?
kohomada mehka?

Customer: Yes, that's nice. Can I try it on?
ov ehka hondai mama mehka aendala balaannada?

Shopkeeper: Good, there's the changing room over there.
hondai, athana thieyenava andhum maarukarana kaamaraya.

Customer: Thank you.
oyaata isthuthiyi.

Shopkeeper:	How does it fit? **kohomada eka hariyanawada?**
Customer:	It's far too large. Do you have the large size? **eka hungak lokui, oyaalagaawe thiyenavada loku 'size' eka.**
Shopkeeper:	Yes, here you are. **ov, menna thiyenava.**
Customer:	Thank you. I'll have it, please. **oyaata isthuthiyi, karunaakarala mata eka denna.**
Shopkeeper:	OK, how would you like to pay? **hondai, kohomada mehkata salli gawanneh?**
Customer:	Do you take credit cards? **oyaa 'credit card' gannawada?**
Shopkeeper:	Yes, we take Visa, Master Card and American Express. **ov, api gannava Visa, Master card saha 'American Express'.**
Customer:	OK, here's my Visa. **hondai. menna mageh 'Visa card' eka.**
Shopkeeper:	Thank you. **oyaata isthuthiyi.**

LESSON 64

Conversation (9) – Shopping For Vegetables

Vendor: What vegetables would you like?
Oyaata o'na mona elawaluda?

Customer: *(points at one)* how much does this vegetable cost?
keeyada meh elawalu ganana?

Vendor: It costs Rs. 200 per kilo
ehka kilo ekak rupiyal desiyak venawa

Customer: How much do the drumsticks cost?
murunga keeyada?

Vendor: Rs.250 for half kilo.
ehka kilo bhageh rupiyal desiya panahai.

Vendor: Would you like egg plant and spinach?
They are very fresh.
oyaa kaemathida wambotu haa nivithi kolawalata, ewa honda aluth.

Customer: No, I would like to get a kilo each of the beans, potatoes and onions.
nehe, mama kaemathi ganna bohnchi, ala saha, lunu kilo ekak.

Vendor: Will that be all?
echcharada okkoma?

Customer:	No, I would like some fruits as well. **nehe, mata thava palathuru tikakuth o'na.**
Vendor:	There are ripe tasty mangoes, bananas, red apples, wood apple, pineapple and green papaw. What would you like? **meh thiyenneh hondata rasa amba kesel, raththu apple, annasie, gaslabu, monawada oyaata o'na?**
Customer:	Please give me a kilo each of all the fruits except the papaw. **mata denna hama ekenma kilo eka gananeh gaslabu nathiwa.**
Vendor:	Here you are, your bill is Rs 2,500. **menna oyaata okkotama rupiyal dedahas pansiyak.**
Customer:	Here's three thousand Rupees. **menna salli rupiyal thundahasak.**
Vendor:	Here is the balance of five hundred Rupees. **menna ethuru salli rupiyal pansiyayak.**
Customer:	Thank you very much. **oyaata hungak isthuthiyi.**

LESSON 65

Conversation (10) – Making A Doctor's Appointment

Patient: Hello. This is Stephen. I'd like to make an appointment to see Dr. Perera.
hello, mama Stephen. mata dosthara perera hamba wenna welawak denna puluwanda?

Receptionist: Certainly. When would you like to see him?
aeththama pluwan. Oyaata kawadada eyawa hamba wenna o'neh?

Patient: Anytime tomorrow morning would be fine.
heta ude, onema velawak hondai.

Receptionist: How about 10 AM?
ude dahaya kohomada?

Patient: That sounds fine. Thank you.
eh welaava hondai. bohoma isthuthiyi.

Receptionist: See you tomorrow morning Mr. Stephen.
api ehenam heta ude hambuwemu Stephen mahaathmaya.

LESSON 66

Conversation (11) – Seeing The Doctor

Doctor: Hello Stephen, What can I do for you?
ayubowan Stephen. Monowada mata karanna puluwan oyaata?

Patient: Good morning Dr. Perera. I have a terrible ache in my lower back.
suba udasanak dosthara Perera. Mata thiyenava harima thada vaedanawak konda pitupasayata hariyen.

Doctor: How long has this been bothering you?
kochchara kaaleka edan meh amaaruwa oyaata thiyenavada?

Patient: I've been having the pain for about the last 3 weeks.
mata meh amaaruwa sumana thunaka withara endam thiyenawa.

Doctor: Do you have any history of back problems?
oyaata meeta kalin ehema konde amaruwa ehema thibila thiyenawada?

Patient: No.
nehe.

Doctor: Are you taking any medications at the moment?
oyaa meh dawaswala monavahari beheth jathi gannawada?

Patient	No. **nehe.**

Doctor:	Okay, let's look at your back. This is muscular. Take these painkillers and come and see me in three days. **hondai, balamu oyaageh konda pitipassa, meh ekka mas pinduwala ridimak.** **oyaata meh wedanashaka beheth pethi paavichchukaranna. dawas thunakin nawatha mawa hambawenna enna.**

Patient:	OK, doctor. Thank you very much. **hondai dosthara mahaathmaya. oyaata bohoma isthuthiyi.**

Doctor:	And remember not to do any strenuous work that will hurt the back. **mathakathiya ganna mahansiwela karana vaeda nokaranna, nathinam konda hondata redaeyi.**

Patient:	Thank you, Doctor **isthuthiyi, dosthara mahaaththaya.**

LESSON 67

Conversation (12) – Making Acquaintance

Rishon: Hi, how are you?
aayubowan, kohomada ethin oyaata?

Ryan: I am fine, thank you.
mata hondai, isthuthiyi.

Rishon: Are you from around here?
oyaa meh langa patha kenekda?

Ryan: Yes, I am from this area, what about you?
ov, mama langa pathamayi, kohomada oyaa?

Rishon: I am on holiday here from Brisbane in Australia.
mama meh niwaduwakata aava 'Australia'weh 'Brisbane' endala.

Ryan: That's great, have you been to many places?
hungak hondai, oyaa hungak pradesha balaanna giyada?

Rishon: Not really but I could do with some help.
ethenma nei namuth mata puluwan yanna thawa kageh hari udawwen.

Ryan:	I am free on Friday if you need to go sight seeing. **oyaata lassana thaen balaanna yanna o'nanam mata sikuradha mukuth nehe.**
Rishon:	Oh, that's wonderful; would you like to join me for lunch today? **ov, eka hungak hondai, oyaa kaemathida mamath eka dawal kaema kanna ekathuwenna.**
Ryan:	Yes, most certainly. **ov, eka hungak esthirayi.**
Rishon:	Do you know of any good restaurant nearby? **oyaa danawada mehariye (langapatha) honda 'restaurant' ekak thiyenethanak?**
Ryan:	Of course. Lucky restaurant is just next door, and they serve very delicious food. **eththatama ov, alhappuwaththeh thiyenava 'lucky restaurant', hungak hondai kaemath harima rassayi.**
Rishon:	OK, let's go there. **hondai ekata yamu.**
Rishon:	*(at the restaurant)* What would you like to eat, buriyani or fried rice? **oyaa monawada kanna kaemathi 'buriyani' da 'fried rice' da?**

Ryan: I would like biriyani.
mama kaemathi 'buriyani'.

Rishon: What drink would you prefer?
oyaa bonna kaemathi, mona beemada?

Ryan: I would like some orange juice. Thanks.
mama kaemathi 'orange juice'. bohoma isthuthiyi.

Rishon: Where do you work?
oyaa koheda vaeda karanneh?

Ryan: Just across the road, at the Bank.
paren ehapaththeh thiyenna, bankuwek.

Rishon: At what time have you got to get back?
oyaa kiyatada apasu ethanata yanna o'na?

Ryan: I have to be there before 2PM.
mama ethanata yanna o'nen dawal dekata kalin.

Rishon: I hope you enjoyed the lunch, it was nice meeting you.
mama sithanawa, oyaa dawal kaema kaala sathutu wuna kiyala. hungak hondai oyaawa hamuwima.

Ryan: Same here.
matath ehemayi.

Rishon: Here is my telephone number. You
can call me when you get home so
that we could discuss about going out
on Friday.
**menna mageh 'telephone'
nambaraya. oyaa gedara gihilla
'call' ekak denna ethokota kaththa
karaganimu sikuraada gamana
gaena**

Ryan: OK, many thanks . See you later
**hondai bohoma isthuthiyi. Passé
hambawemu.**

Rishon: Goodbye.
aayu-bowan.

ANSWERS TO EXERCISES

<u>Lesson 3:</u>

Q2.

මල (flower) ; මළ (dead)

<u>Lesson 4:</u>

Q2. & Q3.

(i)   bring ; gehnavaa ; ගේනවා

(ii) looked ; baeluvaa ; බැලුවා

(iii) wait ; inna ; ඉන්න

(iv) speak ; kataa karanavaa ; කතා කරනවා

(v) love ; aadaraya ; ආදරය

<u>Lesson 5:</u>

Q1.

(i)   mageh paasal nivaaḍuva heṭin avasan

(ii) maṭa uganvanna hoňda guruvaru enavaa nam
     hoňdayi mageh alut pantiyeh.

(iii) alut Sinhala guruvarayaa dakṣa kenek viya yutuyi.

<u>Lesson 7:</u>

Q1.

(i) book ; potha ; පොත

(ii) friend ; miththuraa ; මිතුරා
            yahaluwa ; යහළුවා

(iii) brother ; sahotharayaa ; සහෝදරයා

(iv) duty ; raajakaariya ; රාජකාරිය

(v) home ; gedara ; ගෙදර

(vi) brought ; gena ; ගෙන

(vii) will-go ; yanavaa ; යනවා

Lesson 8:

Q1.

(i) father ; thaaththaa / piyaa ; තාත්තා / පියා

(ii) live ; inna / sajiivi ; ඉන්න / සජීවී

(iii) temple ; pansala ; පන්සල

(iv) name ; nama ; නම

(v) occupation ; rassaava / rakiyyava ; රස්සාව / රැකියාව

(vi) problem ; prasnaya / gaetaluva ; ප්‍රශ්නය / ගැටලුව

(vii) time ; welaawa ; වෙලාව

(viii) children ; lamayi / daruvan ; ළමයි / දරුවන්

(ix) people ; minissu / mahajana ; මිනිස්සු / මහජන

Lesson 9:

Q1.

(i) truth ; aeththa / sathyaya ; ඇත්ත / සත්‍යය

(ii) baby ; lamayi ; ළමයි

(iii) adopt ; hadaagannavaa ; හදාගන්නවා

(iv) continue ; digatama ; දිගටම

(v) told ; kivvaa ; කිව්වා

(vi) understand ; thehrum gannavaa ; තේරුම් ගන්නවා

Lesson 10:

Q1.

(i) shave ; raevula kapanna ; රැවුල කපන්න

(ii) haircut ; koṇḍaya kaepiima ; කොණ්ඩය කැපීම

(iii) beautiful ; lassanayi ; ලස්සනයි

(iv) problem ; gaeṭaluva / amaaruwa ; ගැටලුව / අමාරුව

(v) big ; mahaa / loku ; මහා / ලොකු

Lesson 11:

Q1.

(i) child ; llama ; ළමා
(ii) something ; yamak / mokahari / monovahari ;
                               යමක් / මොකහරි / මොනවහරි
(iii) brush ; burusuva / madhinavaa ; බුරුසුව / මදිනවා
(iv) birth mark ; upan lakuna ; උපන් ලකුණ
(v) long ; digu ; දිගු

Lesson 12:

Q1

(i) cutting ; kaepiima ; කැපීම

(ii) bone ; asthi ; අස්ථි

(iii) hurt ; ridenavaa ; රිදෙනවා

(iv) take care ; balaaganna / pravehsam vanna ;
                              බලාගන්න / ප්‍රවේසම් වන්න

(v) hit ; gaehuuvaa / happuna ; ගැහුවා /හැප්පුනා

(vi) swollen ; idimil-welaa / idimuunhu ;
                          ඉදිමිල් වෙලා / ඉදිමුණු

Lesson 13:

Q1

(i) infection ; aasaadanaya / amaaruwa ;
                          ආසාදනය / අමාරුව
(ii) pain; vehdanaava / ridenavaa ; වේදනාව / රිදෙනවා
(iii) sore ; vanha ; වණ
(iv) cancer ; pillikaavak ; පිළිකාවක්

<u>Lesson 13 (continued)</u>:

Q2

(i)   එයාට පපුවේ අමාරුවක් තියෙනව

(ii)   එයාට තනයේ පිළිකාවක් තියෙනව

(iii)   එයාගේ වකුගඩුව ගල් තිබුන

(iv)   එයාට පිටේ අමාරුවක් තියෙනව

(v)   එයාගේ පස්ස රිදෙනව

<u>Lesson 14</u>:

Q1.

(i) patient ; rohgiah ; රෝගියා

(ii) stones ; gal ; ගල්

(iii) wrong ; vaeradi ; වැරදි

(iv) weak ; durvala ; දුර්වල

(v) operation ; meheyum ; මෙහෙයුම්

Q2.

(i)   එයා හදවත් රෝගියෙක්

(ii)   එයාට අක්මාවේ පිළිකාවක් තියෙනව

(iii)   එයාගේ වකුගඩුව ගල් තිබුන

(iv)   (ඔයාගේ) බඩේ අමාරුවක් තියෙනවද ?

(v)   එයාගේ පෙන හෙල්ල දුරුවලයි

(vi)   එයාගේ ගර්භාසයේ සැත්කමක් කලා

Q3.

A7; B6; C4; D9; E12; F3; G5; H2; I11; J8; K1; L10

Lesson 15:

Q1.

(i) keep ; tabaa ganna ; තබා ගන්න

(ii) uncomfortable ; apahasuyi ; අපහසුයි

(iii) close ; samiipa / vahanna; සමීප / වහන්න

(iv) bring ; gehnavaa ; ගේනවා

(v) bottom ; patuleh ; පතුලේ

(vi) closer ; samiipayi ; සමීපයි

(vii) open ; vivṛta / arinna; විවෘත / අරින්න

Q2.

(i)   පුටුවේ වාඩි වෙන්න

(ii)   මේසය උඩ තියන්න

(iii) මේ ඇඳ මට අපහසුයි

(iv)   (ලියන) මේස දෙක ලඟින් තියන්න

(v)   අර කුඩා බංකුව මෙහාට ගේන්න

(vi)   (එක්ක) පහල තට්ටුවේ තියන්න

(vii) අර දොර වහන්න

(viii) ජනෙල් අරින්න

Lesson 16:

Q1.

(i) hat ; thoppia ; තොප්පිය

(ii) bought ; miladii gaththaa ; මිලදී ගත්තා

(iii) colour ; varnha / paata ; වර්ණ / පාට

(iv) garden ; waththa ; වත්ත

(v) flower ; mala ; මල

(vi) dog ; ballaa ; බල්ලා

(vii) jumped ; paennaa ; පැන්නා

(viii) fence ; vaeta ; වැට

<u>Lesson 16 (continued):</u>

Q2.

(i) මම සුදු තොප්පියක් ගත්තා

(ii) කලුපාට ලස්සනයි

(iii) එයා නිල් පාටට සාරියක් ඇන්දා

(iv) වත්ත හොන්දටම කොළ පාටයි

(v) එයා රතු එළිය පත්තු වුනාට වාහනය
     නැවැත්තුවේ නෑ

(vi) පාට ලස්සන කහ මලක්

(vii) දුඹුරු බල්ලා වැට උඩින් පැන්නා

(viii) රෝස පාට ඇදුම එයාට හුඟක් හොඳයි

(ix) මම දම් පාට කැමති

<u>Lesson 17:</u>

Q1.

(i)   sir ; mahathmaya ; මහත්මයා

(ii) brother ; sahodaraya ; සහෝදරයා

(iii) hospitality ; aagantuka sathkaarayaa ;
                       ආගන්තුක සත්කාරයා

(iv) wish ; suba-pathanawa ; සුබ පතනවා

(v) wedding ; vivaaha ; විවාහ

Q2.

(i) සුබ උදෑසනක් මහත්මයා

(ii) සුබ රාතිරියක් වේවා

(iii) කොහෝමද සහෝදරයා?

(iv) මම ස්තුති කරනවා

(v) ඔයාගේ සත්කාරයට මම බොහොම ස්තුති කරනවා

(vi) ඔයාට සුබ උපන් දිනයක් පතනවා

(vii) ඔයාට සුබ සංවත්සරයක් පතනවා

(viii) සුබ පනස්වෙනි විවාහ සංවත්සරයක් වේවා

<u>**Lesson 18:**</u>

Q1

(i) please ; karunaakara ; කරුණාකර

(ii) soon ; ikmanin ; ඉක්මනින්

(iii) home ; gedara ; ගෙදර

(iv) short ; ketti ; කෙටි

 (v) route ; maargaya ; මාර්ගය

(vi) fast ; ikmanin ; ඉක්මනින්

(vii) fence ; vaeta ; වැට

(viii) now ; daen ; දැන්

Q2

(i) කරුණාකරල ඉක්මනට එන්න

(ii) ඔයා ගෙදර යන්න

(iii) කෙටි පාරෙන් යන්න

(iv) ඉක්මනට ඇවිදින්න

(v) මම දුවන් යනවා

(vi) වැටට උඩින් පනින්න

(vii) මෙතන නවත්වන්න

(viii) දැන් පටන් ගන්න

Q3.

A3; B2; C4; D5; E1

Lesson 19:

Q1.

(i) go ; yanna ; යන්න

(ii) turn ; haerenavaa ; හැරෙනවා

(iii) live ; sajiivi / inneh ; සජීවී / ඉන්නේ

(iv) side ; paeththa ; පැත්ත

(v) sun ; hiru ; හිරු

(vi) rises ; naginava / ihala yayi ; නගිනවා / ඉහල යයි

(vii) sets ; basinava ; බසිනවා

Q2.

(i) කෙලින් යන්න

(ii) දකුණට හැරෙන්න

(iii) වමට හැරෙන්න

(iv) උඩට යන්න

(v) පහලට යන්න

(vi) අපි පදින්චි වෙලා ඉන්නේ දකුණ පත්තේ

(vii) යාපණය තියෙන්නේ ශ්‍රී ලංකාවේ උතුරේ

(viii) හිරු නගින්නේ නැගෙනහිරෙන්

(ix) හිරු බසින්නේ බටහිරෙන්

Lesson 20:

Q1.

(i) occupation ; raekiyaava / rassaawa ; රැකියාව / රස්සාව

(ii) how many ; keedenek ; කීදෙනෙක්

(iii) older ; vaeḍihiṭi ; වැඩිහිටි

(iv) younger ; baala ; බාල

<u>**Lesson 20 (continued):**</u>

Q2.

(i) ඔයාගේ තාත්තාගේ රස්සාව මොකක්ද?

(ii) ඔයාගේ අම්ම කොහෙද ඉන්නේ?

(iii) මේ ඔයාගේ පුතාද?

(iv) ඔයාට දුවල කීදෙනෙක් ඉන්නවද?

(v) ඔයාගේ වැඩිමහල් අක්කාගේ වයස කීයද?

(vi) ඔයාගේ බාල නංගි මොනවද කරන්නේ?

(vii) එයා ඔයාගේ අයියාද?

(viii) ඔයාට මල්ලිලා කී දෙනෙක් ඉන්නවද?

<u>**Lesson 21:**</u>

Q1.

(i) work ; vaedha / kaaryaya ; වැඩ / කාර්යය

(ii) here ; methana ; මෙතන

(iii) nice ; lassanayi ; ලස්සනයි

(iv) lived ; jeevath wunaa ; ජීවත් වුණා

Q2.

(i) ඔයාගේ මාමා කවුද ?

(ii) ඔයාගේ නැන්දා ඉන්නේ කොහෙද ?

(iii) ඔයාගේ නෑනා කොහෙද වැඩ කරන්නේ ?

(iv) ඔයාගේ මස්සිනා හොඳ කෙනෙක් වාගේ

(v) ඔයාගේ සියා මෙතන ඉන්නවද ?

(vi) ඔයාගේ ආච්චි ඔයත් එක්ක ජීවත් වෙනවද ?

Lesson 22:

Q1.

(i) came ; aavaa ; ආවා

(ii) united ; eksath ; එක්සත්

(iii) died ; miiya giyaa / malla ; මිය ගියා / මළ

(iv) beautiful ; lassanayi ; ලස්සනයි

(v) loves ; aadaraya karayi ; ආදරය කරයි

(vi) lot ; godak; ගොඩක්

Q2.

(i) සුනිල් , එයාගේ ස්වාමිපුරුෂයා (මහත්තයා)

(ii) සුරාජ්, එයාගේ බිරිඳ එක්ක ආවේ

(iii) ඔවුන් එකමුතු පවුලක්

(iv) ඔවුන්ගේ මාමාන්ඩි මෙහෙ ජීවත් වෙනවා

(v) එයාගේ නැන්දම්මා ගිය අවුරුද්දේ මැරුණා

(vi) පියදාසට ලස්සන මිණිබිරියන් දෙදෙනෙක්
   ඉන්නවා

Lesson 23:

Q1.

(i) going ; yanavaa ; යනවා

(ii) another ; thavath ; තවත්

(iii) need ; avaśyayi ; අවශ්‍යයි

(iv) give ; denavaa ; දෙනවා

(v) letter ; lipiya ; ලිපිය

(vi) will write ; liyanu aetha ; ලියනු ඇත

Lesson 23 (continued):

Q2.

(i) මම තැපැල් කන්තෝරුවට යන්නව

(ii) මට තව ලියුමක් ලියන්න ඕනේ

(iii) කරුණාකර, මේ පාර්සලය තැපැල් කරන්න

(iv) කරුණාකර , මට රුපියල් පනහේ මුද්දර තුනක් දෙන්න

(v) කරුණාකර, මට ලියුමක් ලියපද්දින්වි කිරිමටට මුද්දර දෙන්න

(vi) මම, ලිපිනය, ලියුම් කවරයේ ලියන්නම්

Lesson 24:

Q1.

(i) caught ; allaa gaththaa ; අල්ලා ගත්තා

(ii) beyond ; obbaṭa ; ඔබ්බට

(iii) look ; balanna ; බලන්න

(iv) going ; yanavaa ; යනවා

Q2.

(i) ඇතුලට යන්න

(ii) එළියට එන්න

(iii) ඔය අතර මැදට අහුවෙලා

(iv) එක ගේට්ටුවෙන් එහා පැත්තේ තියෙන්න

(v) පහල තට්ටුවේ ගිහින් බලාන්න

(vi) මම යනවා උඩ තට්ටුවට

(vii) අපිට පහල තට්ටුවට යන්න ඕන

<u>Lesson 25:</u>

Q1.

(i) nation ; jaathiya ; ජාතිය

(ii) heart ; hadawatha ; හදවත

(iii) corner ; kellavareh ; කෙළවරේ

(iv) medal ; padakkama ; පදක්කම

(v) side ; paeththa ; පැත්ත

(vi) lucky number ; vasanaavantha aṁkaya ; වසනාවන්ත අංකය

(vi) church ; palliya ; පල්ලිය

(vii) planet ; grahalohkaya ; ග්‍රහලෝකය

(viii) commandments ; aagnaavan ; ආඥාවන්

Q2.

(i) එකම රට එකම ජාතිය

(ii) හදවත් දෙක එකමුතුයි

(iii) හතරැස් කොටුවකට කොන් හතරක් තියෙනවා

(iv) මොහාන් පදක්කම් පහක් දිනුව

(v) දාදු කැටයට පැති හයක් තියෙනවා

(vi) හත සුබ ඉලක්කමක් ද?

(vii) මේ නගරයේ පල්ලි අටක් තියෙනවා

(viii) ග්‍රහලෝක නවයක් මිනිසුන්ට බලපායි

(ix) දෙවියන්ගේ දස අනපනත් අනුගමනය කරන්න

<u>Lesson 26:</u>

Q1.

(i) plus ; ekathu kirima ; එකතු කිරීම

(ii) less ; adu kirima ; අඩු කිරීම

(iii) greater ; vaedi ; වැඩි

(iv) odd ; amuthu ; අමුතු

(v) even ; pava ; පව

(vi) dozen ; dusimak ; දුසිමක්

Lesson 26 (continued):

Q2.

(i) දහයට එකක් එකතු කලාම , එකොලහයි

(ii) පහළවෙන් පහක් අඩු කලාම දහයයි

(iii) දොළහා , දාහතරට වඩා අඩුයි

(iv) දාසය , දහතුනට වඩා වැඩියි

(v) දාහත , ඔත්තේ ඉලක්කමක්

(vi) දහය, ඉරට්ටේ ඉලක්කමක්

(vii) දුසිමක් කියන්නේ දොළහක්

Lesson 27:

Q1.

(i) makes ; karai ; කරයි

(ii) times ; vaara ; වාර

(iii) into ; vetha ; වෙත

(iv) means ; yannen adahas veh ; යන්නෙන් අදහස් වේ

(v) century ; siyavasa ; සියවස

(vi) but ; eheth ; එහෙත්

Q2.

(i) දහයයි , දහයයි එකතුව විස්සයි

(ii) විස්ස දෙකෙන් වැඩිකරාම හතලියයි

(iii) අසුවෙන් තිහක් අඩු කරාම පනහයි

(iv) සීය පහෙන් බෙදුවම විස්සයි

(v) සීයක් කියන්නේ ශතකයක්

(vi) තිස්හය සහ හතලිස්දෙක එකතුකරාම කීයද?

(vii) හත් වරක් හත නෙමෙයි , නමුත් හත් වරක්
    හැත්තෑව

Lesson 29:

Q1.

(i) percent ; pratiśathaya ; ප්‍රතිශතය

(ii) runs ; duvanavaa ; දුවනවා

(iii) old ; paeranhi ; පැරණි

(iv) ago ; vayasa ; වයස

(v) students ; sisu ; සිසු

(vi) sold ; vikuṇhuvaa ; විකුණුවා

(vii) collection ; ekathu ; එකතු

(viii) nearly ; aasanna ; ආසන්න

(ix) talking ; kathaa karanavaa ; කතා කරනවා

Q2.

(i) සියට එකසිය පණහක ප්‍රතිශතයක්

(ii) ලකුණු දෙසිය විස්සයි

(iii) අවුරුදු දෙසියක් පරනයි

(iv) අවුරුදු භාරසියකට කලින් (ඉස්සර)

(v) (සිසුන්) ලමයි හයසියක් සිටිනවා

(vi) ප්‍රවේශ පත්‍ර හත්සියක් විකුණලා

(vii) එකතුව (dollar) දහකට කිට්ටුයි

(viii) අපි කතා කරන්නේ දහස් ගණනින්

Lesson 30:

Q1.

(i) many ; bohoh ; බොහෝ

(ii) more ; thava ; තව

(iii) migrated ; saṁkramaṇaya viya ; සංක්‍රමණය විය

(iv) countries ; raṭaval ; රටවල්

<u>**Lesson 31:**</u>

Q1.

(i) children ; lamayi / daruvan ; ළමයි / දරුවන්

(ii) born ; upannaa ; උපන්නා

(iii) family ; pavulak ; පවුලක්

(iv) arrive ; aaveh / paemineh ; ආවේ / පැමිණේ

(v) receives ; labuna (laebeh) ; ලැබේ

(vi) race ; jaathiya ; ජාතිය

(vii) agenda ; nyaaya patraya ; න්‍යාය පත්‍රය

Q2.

(i) ළමයි පස් දෙනගෙන්, පල වෙනි තුන්දෙනා පිරිමි - ළමයි

(ii) මම පවුලේ හතර - වෙනිය

(iii) පස්වෙනියට ආවේ 'Silva'

(iv) තඹ පදක්කම ලැබුනේ තුන්වෙනි තැනට

(v) දිවීමේ තරගයෙන් "Sunil" දෙවෙනියට ආවා

(vi) ඔහු පන්තියේ පලවෙනිය

(vii) වැඩසටහනේ හත්වෙනියට තියෙන්නේ මොකක්ද ?

<u>Lesson 32:</u>

Q1.

(i) now ; daen ; දැන්

(ii) show ; darshanaya / penvanna; දර්ශනය / පෙන්වන්න

(iii) start ; patan gannava ; පටන් ගන්නවා

aaramba karanna ; ආරම්භ කරන්න

(iv) coming ; enavaa ; එනවා

(v) always ; nitharama / saemaviṭama; නිතරම / සෑමවිටම

(vi) match ; kriidaawa / tharangaya; ක්‍රීඩාව / තරඟය

(vii) better ; vadaa honda ; වඩා හොඳ

(viii) early ; kalin / mul; කලින් / මුල්

(ix) watch ; oralohsuwa ; ඔරලෝසුව

(x) fast ; vadyi / ikmanin ; වඩියි / ඉක්මනින්

<u>Lesson 33:</u>

Q1.

(i) today ; ada ; අද

(ii) meeting ; hambavenawa ; හම්බවෙනවා

raesweema ; රැස්වීම

(ii) tomorrow ; heta ; හෙට

(iv) answer ; pillithuru ; පිළිතුරු

(v) hide ; hanganna / sangavanna ; හංගන්න / සඟවන්න

(vi) consider ; ithanawa ; ඉතනව

salakaa balanna ; සලකා බලන්න

(vii) carefully ; pravehśamen ; ප්‍රවේශමෙන්

(viii) wrong ; vaeradi ; වැරදි

Lesson 34:

Q1.

(i) rains ; vaesi ; වැසි

(ii) busy ; hondatama vaeda ; හොඳටම වැඩ

(iii) overseas ; pitarata / videhśiya ; පිටරට / විදේශීය

(iv) birthday ; upan dinaya ; උපන් දිනය

(v) cold ; siithalai ; සීතලයි

(vi) anniversary ; sangvathsaraya ; සංවත්සරය

(vii) mid ; maeda ; මැද

(viii) holidays ; nivaadu ; නිවාඩු

(ix) around ; tharameh / avata ; තරමේ / අවට

Q2.

පාසල් සඳහා නත්තල් නිවාඩුව නොවැම්බර් අවසන් සතියේ ආරම්භ වේ.

paasal saňdahaa naththal nivaaḍuva novaembar avasan sathiyeh aaramha veh.

Lesson 35:

Q1.

(i) holiday ; nivaadu / davasak ; නිවාඩු / දවසක්

(ii) someone ; kenek ; කෙනෙක්

(iii) night; raae; රෑ

(iv) flights ; guwan gaman ; ගුවන් ගමන්

(v) lunch ; dawal kemata ; දවල් කෑමට
         divaa aahaaraya ; දිවා ආහාරය

(vi) next ; iilanga ; ඊළඟ

(vii) visitors ; amuththu waagaya ; අමුත්තු වාගය
         amuththan ; අමුත්තන්

Lesson 36:

Q1.

(i) works ; vaeda karanneh ; වැඩකරන්නේ

(ii) appointment ; hamuvenna velaavak ;
හමුවෙන්න වෙලාවක්

(iii) consult ; upades ganna ; උපදෙස් ගන්න

(iv) hospital ; ispirithaaleh ; ඉස්පිරිතාලේ

(v) brilliant ; athi-daksha ; අති දක්ෂ

(vi) yesterday ; iiyeh ; ඊයේ

Q2.

(i) එයා හොඳ ගුරු වරයෙක්

(ii) මම පූජකවරයෙක් බලාන්න ඕනේ

(iii) 'Ramana' ඉනජිනේරු විදයට වැඩ කරන්නේ

(iv) මට දොස්තර හමුවෙන්න වෙලාවක් තියෙනවා

(v) මට මගේ නීතිඥයාගෙන් උපදේස් ගන්න ඕනේ

(vi) ඉස්පිත්තාලේ ප්‍රධාන හෙදිය 'Susan'

(vii) 'John' සාමන්‍ය ලිපිකරුවෙක්

(viii) 'Peter' අති දක්ෂ ගණකාදිකාරයෙක්

(ix) ඊයෙ පොලිසිය 'Suraj' ව අත් අඩංගුවට ගත්තා

Lesson 37:

Q1.

(i) stop ; navathvanna ; නවත්වන්න

(ii) freedom ; nidahasa ; නිදහස

(iii) poisonous ; visakaru ; විසකරු

(iv) snake ; naya / sarpayaa ; නයා / සර්පයා

(v) plan ; kumantranaya ; කුමන්ත්‍රණය

(vi) president ; janadhipathi ; ජනාධිපති

Lesson 38:

Q1.

(i) longtime ; goda (ligu) kaalaya ; දිගු කාලය

(ii) adore ; aadarey ; ආදරේ

(iii) laid ; taebuuha ; තැබුහ

(iv) eggs ; biththara ; බිත්තර

(v) lot ; godak ; ගොඩක්

(vi) please ; karunaakara ; කරුණාකර

(vii) apply ; gaaganna ; ගාගන්න

(viii) torturing ; vada denavaa ; වද දෙනවා

(ix) pet ; surathal / satha ; සුරතල් / සතා

(x) favourite ; priyathama ; ප්‍රියතම

Lesson 39:

Q1.

(i) mother ; ammah (mava) ; අම්මා (මව)

(ii) every ; haema (saaema) ; හැම (සෑම)

(iii) cart ; karaththaya ; කරත්තය

(iv) pull ; adinna ; අදින්න

(v) tasty ; rasavath ; රසවත්

(vi) filthy ; jaraava (apirisidu) ; ජරාව (අපිරිසිදු)

(vii) road ; paara ; පාර

(viii) house ; gedara (nivasa) ; ගෙදර (නිවස)

(ix) forest ; kaelaaeva (vana) ; කැලෑව (වන)

(x) bathe ; naanavaa ; නානවා

(xi) zoo ; saththuwaththa ; සත්තුවත්ත

(xii) and ; saha ; සහ

Lesson 40:

Q1.

(i) garden; waththa ; වත්ත

(ii) webs ; makuludael ; මකුළුදැල්

(iii) wall ; biththiya ; බිත්තිය

(iv) pond ; pokunha ; පොකුණ

(v) everywhere ; haemathaenama ; හැමතැනම

(vi) jungle ; kaeleh ; කැලේ

Lesson 41:

Q1.

(i) get me ; maava ganna ; මාව ගන්න

(ii) keep ; thienna (thabaa ganna) ; තබා ගන්න

(iii) give me ; maṭa denna ; මට දෙන්න

(iv) food ; aahaara ; ආහාර

(v) will eat ; kannam ; කන්නම්

Lesson 42:

Q1.

(i) taste ; rasa ; රස

(ii) favourite ; piriyathama ; ප්‍රියතම

(iii) vegetables ; eḷavaḷu ; එළවළු

(iv) heart ; hadavatha ; හදවත

(v) cooking ; uyanava ; උයනව

(vi) need ; avashyayi ; අවශ්‍යයි

(vii) here ; mehe (methana) ; මෙතන

(viii) readily available ; ඇතිවෙන්න තියෙනව

Lesson 43:

Q1.

(i) buy ; miladii ganna ; මිලදී ගන්න

(ii) expensive ; godak ganan ; ගොඩක් ගණන්

(iii) health ; saukhyaya ; සෞඛ්‍යය

(iv) fruit ; palathuru ; පලතුරු

(v) season ; wareh ; වාරේ

(vi) milk ; kiri ; කිරි

Q2.

(i) මම අද කොහොමහරි දොඩම් ටිකක් ගන්න ඕනේ

(ii) මිදී ගොඩක් ගණන්

(iii) ශරීර සෞඛ්‍යයට ඇපල් හොඳයි

(iv) මගේ ප්‍රියතම පලතුර කෙසෙල්

(v) මේ අඹ වාරේ නොවේ

(vi) ඕනේම 'curry' එකට පොල්කිරි එකතු කරාම
     රස වැඩි වෙනවා

Lesson 44:

Q1.

(i) generally ; saamaanya (poduveh) ; පොදුවේ

(ii) most people ; bohoh minisun ; බොහෝ මිනිසුන්

(iii) both ; dekema ; දෙකම

(iv) exports ; apanayana ; අපනයන

(v) tastier ; vadhaath rasavath ; වඩාත් රසවත්

<u>Lesson 45:</u>

Q1.

(i) preparation ; hadhapu vidiya ; හදපු විදිය

(ii) delicious ; honda rasayi ; හොඳ රසයි

(iii) prefer ; vadaa kaemathi ; වඩා කැමති

(iv) friend ; mithuraa (yahaluwaa);මිතුරා (යහලුවා)

(v) eat ; kanna ; කන්න

(vi) cooks ; uyanavaa ; උයනවා

Q2.

(i) මේ හරක් මස් හදපු විදිය හොඳ රසයි

(ii) මෙය හරක් මස් සකස් කිරීමකි

(iii) මම එළු-මස් 'curry' එකට වඩා කැමති බැටළු-
      මස් 'curry' එකට

(iv) මගේ යහළුවා හරක් මස් කන්නේ නෑ

(v) හුඟක් මිනිස්සු ඌරු මස් කන්නේ නෑ

(vi) මගේ අම්මා හුඟක් රස්සට කුකුළ් මස් උයනවා

<u>Lesson 46:</u>

Q1.

(i) borrow ; ganna ; ගන්න

(ii) give me ; mata denna ; මට දෙන්න

(iii) need ; o'ne ; ඕනේ

(iv) paper ; kadhadasi ; කඩදාසි

(v) get yourself ; ganna o'ne ; ගන්න ඕනේ

Q2.

(i) මට ඔයාගේ පෑන ගන්න පුලුවන්ද

(ii) මට මකනය දෙන්න

(iii) අපිට 'stapler' එකක් ඕනේ

(iv) ඔයාට කඩදාසි ඕන වෙනවා

(v) ඔයා පැන්සල් 'sharpener' එකක් ගන්න ඕන

Lesson 47:

Q1.

(i) bought ; miladii gaththaa ; මිලදී ගත්තා

(ii) received ; laebuna ; ලැබුනා

(iii) transaction ; huwamaaruwa ; හුවමාරුව

(iv) high ; hungak ; හුඟක්

(vi) big ; loku ; ලොකු

Q2.

(i) මම මේක හරි ලාබෙට මිලදී ගත්තා

(ii) මට හොඳ මිල අඩුකිරීමක් ලැබුන

(iii) මම මේ හුවමාරුවට කොමිස් මුදලක් ගෙව්වා

(iv) මේ හුවමාරුවට 'broker' ගස්තුව හුඟක් වැඩියි

(v) මම ඒ 'charity' එකට ලොකු දැන් දිස්මක් කලා

Lesson 48:

Q1.

(i) attended ; giya ; ගියා

(ii) many ; keepaya ; කීපය

(iii) road ; paara ; පාර

(iv) far ; dura ; දුර

(v) lecturer ; kathikaacaarya ; කථිකාචාර්ය

(vi) very big ; godak loku ; ගොඩක් ලොකු

<u>Lesson 48 (continued)</u>:

Q2.

(i) මම විදුහල් දෙකකට ගියා

(ii) මෙහේ රෙපරමාදු ආගමේ පල්ලි කීපයක් මම දකිනවා

(iii) මේ පාර අන්තිමට බෞද්ධ පන්සලක්
තියෙනවා

(iv) පොලිස් ඉස්තානයට මෙතන සිට ගොඩක්
දුරයි

(v) 'Kusuma' කොළඹ විශ්ව විත්‍යාලේ කතාවාර්ය
වාරියක්

(vi) අපිට ගොඩක් ලොකු ගුවන් තොටුපලක්

<u>Lesson 49</u>:

Q1.

(i) last week ; giya sumaaneh; ගිය සුමානෙන්

(ii) from here ; methana indala; මෙතන ඉදල

(iii) arriving ; pamin enawa ; පමින් එනවා
godabahinawa ; ගොඩබහිනවා

(iv) enjoyed ; sathutu wuna ; සතුටු වුණා
santhosha wuna ; සන්තොෂ වුණා

Q2.

(i) ගියා සුමානේ මම අලුත් car එකක් ගත්තා

(ii) මෙතන ඉදල bus එකක් තියනවද කොළඹට
යන්න

(iii) මගේ සහෝදරයා අද පැමිනෙනවා ගුවන්යානයෙන්

(iv) ර්යේ මම helicopter ride එකෙන් සතුටු වුණා

Lesson 50:

Q1.

(i) small ; kudaa ; කුඩා

(ii) activity ; dewal ; දේවල්

(iii) peaceful ; saamakaami ; සාමකාමී

(iv) culture ; saṁskṛtiya ; සංස්කෘතිය

(v) work ; vaeda ; වැඩ

Q2.

(i) මම හැදි වැඩුනේ කුඩා නගරයක

(ii) රට නගරයේ ගොඩක් විනෝද දේවල්
සිද්ධවෙනය

(iii) අපේ රට ගොඩක් සාමකාමි

(iv) ගම්බද මිනිසුන්ට ඔවුන්තාවෙනික සංස්කෘතියක්
තියෙනවා

(v) ගොඩක් මිනිස්සු නගරබද වැඩ කරන්න
කැමතියි

Lesson 51:

Q1.

(i) front ; issaraha ; ඉස්සරහ

(ii) near ; langa ; ළඟ

(iii) very nice ; godak lassanayi ; ගොඩක් ලස්සනයි

(iv) garden ; waththa ; වත්ත

(v) many ; godak ; ගොඩක්

(vi) weed killer ; val paelaaeti nashaka ;

වල් පැලෑති නාෂක

(vii) wife ; bharyaa; භාර්යා

<u>**Lesson 51 (continued):**</u>

Q2.

(i) ඔයාට ලස්සන ඉස්සරහ වත්තක්
තියෙනවා

(ii) අපේ ගෙදර ළඟ පොදු උද්‍යානයක්
තියෙනවා

(iii) ඒ තනකොල ගොඩක් ලස්සනයි

(iv) ඔයාගේ වත්තේ පැල ගොඩක් තියෙනවා

(v) මට මල් ගොඩක් තියෙනවා

(vi) මට පැල වලට වල් පැළෑති නාෂක ඉහින්න
අවශ්‍යයි

(vii) මම මගේ භාර්යාවට මල් ටිකක් මිල දී ගත යුතුමයි

<u>**Lesson 52:**</u>

Q1.

(i) health ; sawukyaya ; සෞඛ්‍යය
(ii) essential ; athyawashya ; අත්‍යවශ්‍ය
(iii) most ; bohoh (hungak) ; හුඟාක්
(iv) used ; paavichi karanna ; පාවිච්චිකරන්න
(v) flavour ; rasaya ; රසය

Q2.

(i) ගොඩක් කහ සෞඛ්‍යයට හොඳ නැහැ
(ii) ආසියාතික කෑම වලට ඉහුරු අත්‍යවශ්‍යයි
(iii) හුඟාක් ඉන්දියානු කෑමවලට මිරිස් කුඩු යොදනවා
(iv) හුඟාක් ඉන්දියානු කෑමවලට මිරිස් කුඩු
පාවිච්චිකරන්න
(v) 'curry' රසකරන්න කුරුඳ පාවිච්චිකරනවා

191

Lesson 53:

Q1.

(i) happy ; kaemathyi ; කැමති

(ii) government ; aanduwa ; ආණ්ඩුව

(iii) family ; pavulak ; පවුලක්

(iv) freedom ; nidahasa ; නිදහස

(v) stress ; peedaawen ; පීඩාවෙන්

Q2.

(i) මිනිස්සු සතුටුයි

(ii) වත්මන් රජය ගැන ජනතාව සතුටුයි

(iii) පිරිමියා ගහ මූලිකයා

(iv) දැන් කාලේ ළමයින්ට උවමනාවට වඩා නිදහස තියෙනවා

(v) විශ්ව විද්‍යාල වල ශිෂ්‍යන් ගොඩක් පීඩාවෙන් ඉන්නේ

Lesson 54:

Q1.

(i) library ; pusthakaalaya ; පුස්තකාලය

(ii) borrowed ; nhayata gaththa; ණයට ගත්ත

(iii) documents ; liyakiavili ; ලියකියවිලි

(iv) unattended ; kiyawapu naethi ; කියවපු නැති

(v) arrange ; askaranava ; අස්කරනවා

(vi) move ; maarukara ; මාරුකර

(vii) files ; lipigonu ; ලිපිගොනු

(viii) relevant ; adaala ; අදාල

192

<u>Lesson 54 (continued):</u>

Q2.

(i) අපිට හොඳ පුස්තකාලයක් තියෙනවා

(ii) මම ඒ පොත පුස්තකාලයෙන් අරගත්තා

(iii) අර ලියකියවිලි කූඩය ඇතුලට දැම්මා

(iv) අර බන්දේශියේ කියවපු නෑති ලියුම් ගොඩක්
     තියෙනවා

(v) මගේ පොත් රාක්කය පිලිවෙලකට උස් කරන්න
     ඕන

(vi) අපි ලියකියවිලි අල්මාරිය අනිත් කොනට
     මාරුකරමු

(vii) ගේනවා සියලුම ගොනු

(viii) කරුණාකරල අදාල ලිපිගොනු විසුර්ත කරන්න

<u>Lesson 55:</u>

Q1.

(i) speak ; kaththa karanava ; කතා කරනවා

(ii) drive ; ela wanna (pada wanna) ; පදවන්න

(iii) catching ; lung weneva ; ලං වෙනවා

(iv) little ; tikkak ; ටික්කක්

(v) road ; paara ; පාර

Q2.

(i) ඔයා කත්තා කරනව හරි ඉග්මනට

(ii) ටික්කක් වේගයන් එලවන්න

(iii) ඔවුන් හරිම හෙමින් අපිට ළඟ වෙනවා

(iv) ටිකක් හෙමින් පදවන්න

(v) මේ පාරේනම් කොහෙත්ම වේගය වැඩිකරන්න බෑ

ADDITIONAL VOCABULARY

A

accident	–	anathura	–	අනතුර
across	–	harahaa	–	හරහා
adult	–	vaedhihiti	–	වැඩිහිටි
after	–	anathuruva	–	අනතුරුව
again	–	naevatha	–	නැවත
agreed	–	ekaṅga viya	–	එකඟ විය
air	–	guvan	–	ගුවන්
all	–	saema	–	සෑම
		(okkoma)	–	(ඔක්කොම)
alone	–	thaniva	–	තනිව
among	–	athara	–	අතර
amount	–	pramaannaya	–	ප්‍රමාණය
angel	–	devduuva	–	දෙව්දූව
animals	–	sathun	–	සතුන්
answer	–	pillithura	–	පිළිතුර

B

baby	–	ladaruvaa	–	ළදරුවා
		(baba)	–	(බබා)

bad	–	naraka	–	නරක
bag	–	baaegaya	–	බෑගය
bangle	–	vallalu	–	වළලු
bat	–	vavuulaa	–	වවුලා
beach	–	veralla	–	වෙරළ
beat	–	gahanavaa	–	ගහනවා
		(pahara denavaa)	–	(පහර දෙනවා)
belt	–	patiya	–	පටිය
beauty	–	ruupaya	–	රූපය
		(alaṁkaaraya)	–	(අලංකාරය)
before	–	issara	–	ඉස්සර
		(kalin)	–	(කලින්)
blood	–	leh	–	ලේ
body	–	aenga	–	ඇඟ
		(sirura)	–	(සිරුර)
boil	–	unu	–	උනු
bread	–	paan	–	පාන්
breakfast	–	udehkaaema	–	උදේකෑම

C

cap	–	thoppiya	–	තොප්පිය
clap	–	athpudi	–	අත්පුඩි
clean	–	pirisuudu	–	පිරිසුදු
cloth	–	redda	–	රෙද්ද
coffee	–	kohpi	–	කෝපි
colour	–	paata	–	පාට
comb	–	panaava	–	පනාව
common	–	podu	–	පොදු
counter	–	kavuntareh	–	කවුන්ටරේ
cross	–	kurusiya	–	කුරුසිය
cruel	–	napuru	–	නපුරු

D

darkness	–	kaluvara	–	කළුවර
deaf	–	bihiri	–	බිහිරි
delay	–	parakkuva	–	පරක්කුව
desire	–	aasaava	–	ආසාව
devil	–	yakshayaa	–	යක්ෂයා
dinner	–	raaekaema	–	රෑකෑම
dirty	–	apirisidu	–	අපිරිසිදු

disease	–	rohgaya	–	රෝගය
doubt	–	saekaya	–	සැකය
dream	–	sihina	–	සිහින
dress	–	aenduma	–	ඇඳුම

E

eat	–	kanna	–	කන්න
earlier	–	peraatuva	–	පෙරාතුව
end	–	avasaanaya	–	අවසානය
enjoy	–	saepavidinavaa	–	සැපවිදිනවා
entrance	–	aethulveema	–	ඇතුල්වීම
erase	–	makaa damanna	–	මකා දමන්න
escape	–	berenavaa	–	බේරෙනවා
exit	–	pitaviima	–	පිටවීම

F

face	–	muhuna	–	මුහුණ
fail	–	varaddanavaa	–	වරද්දන්නවා
		(asaarthakayi)	–	(අසාර්ථකයි)
faint	–	moorjava	–	මූර්ජව
		(klaantha venavaa)	–	(ක්ලාන්ත වෙනවා)

fan	–	vataapana	–	වටාපන
		(rasikayek)	–	(රසිකයෙක්)
farm	–	govipala	–	ගොවිපල
fat	–	mahatha	–	මහත
		(mehdaya)	–	(මේදය)
feel	–	daenenavaa	–	දැනෙනවා
fence	–	vaeta	–	වැට
festival	–	utsavaya	–	උත්සවය
fever	–	unha	–	උණ
fog	–	miiduma	–	මීදුම
fool	–	mohdhaya	–	මෝඩය
foolish	–	mohdhayi	–	මෝඩයි
full	–	puurnha	–	පූර්ණ

G

gate	–	gehttuva	–	ගේට්ටුව
gem	–	maenhik	–	මැණික්
general	–	saamaanaya	–	සාමානය
		(janaraal)	–	(ජනරාල්)
giddiness	–	karakaevilla	–	කරකැවිල්ල
gift	–	thaaeggak	–	තෑග්ගක්

god	–	devyoh	–	දෙව්යෝ
		(devi)	–	(දෙවි)
gold	–	ran	–	රන්
gravel	–	boraḷu	–	බොරළු
gravy	–	hodi	–	හොදි
ground	–	bima	–	බිම
gun	–	thuvakkuva	–	තුවක්කුව

H

health	–	savukkaya	–	සෞඛ්‍යය
heaven	–	swargaya	–	ස්වර්ගය
heavy	–	bara	–	බර
hell	–	niraya	–	නිරය
hill	–	kaňdukaraya	–	කඳුකරය
honest	–	avanka	–	අවංක
hot	–	unhusum	–	උණුසුම්

I

imagination	–	parikalpanaya	–	පරිකල්පනය
innocent	–	ahiṁsaka	–	අහිංසක
itch	–	kaesiima	–	කැසීම

| insult | – apahaasa karanavaa – | අපහාස කරනවා |

J

jaggery	–	hakuru	–	හකුරු
jam	–	thadabadaya	–	තදබදය
joint	–	ehkaabaddha	–	ඒකාබද්ධ
joke	–	vihiluvak	–	විහිළුවක්

K

king	–	raja	–	රජ
kiss	–	haaduvak	–	හාදුවක්
kitchen	–	kussiya	–	කුස්සිය
know	–	dannavaa	–	දන්නව

L

lake	–	vila	–	විල
lame	–	kora	–	කොර
		(nonndi)	–	(නොණ්ඩි)
lick	–	levekanna	–	ලෙවකන්න
lie	–	boru	–	බොරු
lift	–	osavanna	–	ඔසවන්න
light	–	eliva	–	එලිය

lightening	–	akunu kiriima	–	අකුණු කිරීම
liquor	–	mathpaen	–	මත්පැන්
listen	–	ahanavaa	–	අහනවා
load	–	bara	–	බර
lock	–	agula	–	අගුල
lose	–	naethivenavaa	–	නැතිවෙනවා
loss	–	alaabhaya	–	අලාභය
		(naethiveema)	–	නැතිවීම
lost	–	naethi vunhaa	–	නැතිවුණා
love	–	aadaraya	–	ආදරය
luggage	–	badu	–	බඩු
		(gaman malu)	–	ගමන් මලු

M

matchbox	–	ginipettiya	–	ගිනිපෙට්ටිය
magazine	–	sangaraava	–	සඟරාව
meal	–	kaaema	–	කෑම
memory	–	mathakaya	–	මතකය
method	–	kramaya	–	ක්‍රමය
milk	–	kiri	–	කිරි
mind	–	manasa	–	මනස

minute	–	minithuva	–	මිනිත්තුව
mirror	–	kannaadiya	–	කන්නාඩිය
		(kaeḍapata)	–	(කැඩපත)
moon	–	saňda	–	සඳ
mosquito	–	maduruvaa	–	මදුරුවා
moustache	–	uduraevulla	–	උඩුරැවුල
mud	–	mada	–	මඩ

N

naughty	–	daňgakaara	–	දඟකාර
necklace	–	maalaya	–	මාලය
net	–	vaaela	–	වැල
number	–	ilakkama	–	ඉලක්කම
nurse	–	kirimavu	–	කිරිමවු
		(hediyak)	–	(හෙදියක්)

O

obey	–	kiikaru venava	–	කීකරු වෙනවා
ocean	–	saagaraya	–	සාගරය
offence	–	varadak	–	වරදක්
		(vaeradi kirima)	–	(වැරදි කිරීම)

oil	–	thel	–	තෙල්
old	–	paeranhi	–	පැරණි
once	–	varak	–	වරක්
only	–	ekama	–	එකම
ooze	–	vaessenavaa	–	වැස්සෙනවා
or	–	hoh	–	හෝ
original	–	mul	–	මුල්

P

peace	–	saama	–	සාම
percent	–	prathisathaya	–	ප්‍රතිසතය
		(siyayaṭa)	–	(සියයට)
press	–	obanna	–	ඔබන්න
province	–	pallaatha	–	පළාත
part	–	kotasa	–	කොටස
partner	–	sahakaru	–	සහකරු
partnership	–	sahakaarakama	–	සහකාරකම
		(havulkaaritvaya)	–	(හවුල්කාරිත්වය)
patient	–	rohgiyaa	–	රෝගියා
patience	–	ivasiima	–	ඉවසීම
peel	–	lella	–	ලෙල්ල

| pure | – | pirisudu | – | පිරිසිදු |

Q

queen	–	raejina	–	රැජින
quick	–	ikman	–	ඉක්මන්
quiet	–	nigvala	–	නිග්වල
		(nihanhdayi)	–	(නිහඩයි)
quit	–	pitavenavaa	–	පිටවෙනවා
		(ivath)	–	ඉවත්

R

rag	–	vaerahali	–	වැරහලි
		(redhi kada)	–	(රෙදි කඩ)
rail	–	dumriya	–	දුම්රිය
raise	–	osavanna	–	ඔසවන්න
remember	–	mathakvenavaa	–	මතක්වෙනවා

S

same	–	sama	–	සම
		(ekama)	–	(එකම)
salary	–	padiya	–	පඩිය
sari	–	saari	–	සාරි

scissors	–	kathuru	–	කතුරු
secret	–	rahasa	–	රහස
send	–	yavanna	–	යවන්න
shoe	–	sapaththu	–	සපත්තු
short	–	keti	–	කෙටි
snow	–	hima	–	හිම
sports	–	kriidaa	–	ක්‍රීඩා
stone	–	gal	–	ගල්
sugar	–	siini	–	සීනි
sweet	–	mihiri	–	මිහිරි

T

thick	–	uku	–	උකු
		(ghana)	–	ඝන
things	–	dheval	–	දේවල්
think	–	hithanavaa	–	හිතනවා
		(sithanna)	–	(සිතන්න)
time	–	kaalaya	–	කාලය
tiny	–	chuutti	–	චූටි
truth	–	sathyaya	–	සත්‍යය

U

ugly	–	kaetayi	–	කැතයි
umbrella	–	kudaya	–	කුඩය
unable	–	nohaeki	–	නොහැකි
uncertain	–	anumaana	–	අනුමාන
		(aviniścitha)	–	අවිනිශ්චිත
unclean	–	apirisudu	–	අපිරිසිදු
unfair	–	asaadaranhayi	–	අසාධරණයි
unfit	–	nusudusuya	–	නුසුදුසුය
unity	–	samagiya	–	සමගිය
unless	–	naethahoth	–	නැතහොත්
		(haera)	–	හැර

V

vast	–	ithavishaala	–	ඉතවිශාල
		(viśaalayi)	–	(විශාලයි)
vegetable	–	ellavalhu	–	එළවළු
very	–	bohoh	–	බොහෝ
		(ithaama)	–	ඉතාම
view	–	dhaekma	–	දැක්ම
villain	–	duṣṭayaa	–	දුෂ්ටයා

W

wash	–	sehdiima	–	සේදීම
wasp	–	baṁbra	–	බඹර
water	–	jala	–	ජල
way	–	aakaaraya	–	ආකාරය
weed	–	valpaelaehti	–	වල්පැලෑටි
weak	–	durvala	–	දුර්වල
wind	–	sullanga	–	සුළඟ

X

| x-ray | – | eksreh | – | එස්රේ |

Y

yearly	–	vaarṣikava	–	වාර්ෂිකව
young	–	baala	–	බාලා
		(tharunha)	–	(තරුණ)

Z

zero	–	bandura	–	බඳුර
		(suunya)	–	(සුන්‍ය)
zone	–	kalaapaya	–	කලාපය
zoom	–	viśaalanaya karanna	–	විශාලනය කරන්න